Saints and Parachutes

CHIEF PETTY OFFICER S. J. TUCKWELL G.C.
1941

LIEUTENANT-COMMANDER
JOHN MILLER G.C.

SAINTS
AND PARACHUTES

Two Aspects of an Adventure

"*Venite, audite et narrabo, omnes qui timetis
Dominum: quanta fecit Dominus animae meae.*"

Ps. 65

CONSTABLE   PUBLISHERS   LONDON

LONDON
PUBLISHED BY
Constable and Company Ltd
10-12 ORANGE STREET, W.C.2

INDIA *and* PAKISTAN
Orient Longmans Ltd
BOMBAY   CALCUTTA   MADRAS

CANADA
Longmans, Green and Company
TORONTO

SOUTH *and* EAST AFRICA
Longmans, Green and Company Ltd
CAPETOWN   NAIROBI

First Published 1951

PRINTED IN GREAT BRITAIN BY THE ALCUIN PRESS, WELWYN GARDEN CITY, HERTS

TO CLARE

*who made one half
of these adventures possible*

Contents

Illustrations

---

*The portrait of Chief Petty Officer Tuckwell is reproduced
by kind permission of the National Museum of Wales*

Author's Note

I am ruefully aware that this is rather a strange selection of stories. But it is a first hand account of two sets of adventures and I have written it in the hope that there will be many who are interested in one, even if not in both. The book is arranged in alternate chapters, so that those who care only for the adventures with the parachute-mines can the more easily skip the adventures with the saints. I must make clear that what I have just called "parachute-mines" were the huge mines which the public promptly, though not really correctly, called "land-mines".

I want to thank three people who are not mentioned in the book by name—Lady Arthur Grosvenor, who gave me the great happiness of living in her house in Eaton Square for much of the mining period in London in 1940-41; Lieutenant-Commander Horace Taylor, G.C., the life and soul of "the profession", who was so nearly killed in Birmingham but lived to go chasing mines at the bottom of the sea; and Archie Rose, C.I.E., J.P., of China and Framlingham, who ordered me to write these tales.

I have also to acknowledge the kindness of Messrs. Sheed and Ward, who permitted quotations from E. Allison Peers' *Life of Saint Teresa*.

Nairobi, Kenya Colony.
15 October, 1950

CHAPTER ONE

H.M.S. KING ALFRED
1940

"Quare fremuerunt gentes: et populi meditati sunt inania?"
Ps. 2

H.M.S. *King Alfred*, the R.N.V.R. training
establishment at Hove in Sussex, was really a
municipal swimming-bath. That, and the fact
that it was on the sea-front, was about all the connection
it had with water; but the place provided the necessary
space for preliminary naval training. The training given
was very "preliminary" indeed, and very short, but it
was extremely well done, and the raw recruit to the
Service in 1940 who passed through *King Alfred* had
reason to be grateful.

At the time I joined—August, 1940—the place contained
men of two types: young men who had joined on the
"lower deck" as ratings and had been selected as potential
officers, and older men, with yachting or other experience,
who had been offered direct commissions. I was in the
latter group, and was then aged thirty-seven. Yachting
had been my hobby for at least twenty years, and I knew
some of the south coast waters well. I had volunteered
with an idea that I might be useful in something like a
motor torpedo-boat in the event of an invasion; mean-

while, I proposed to go after mines, though I had little
notion what a mine was and no conception at all that I
should have my wish granted. It was granted in less than
five weeks, and in a most spectacular form.

I arrived at Hove rather breathless. A few days before,
I had received a printed letter from the Admiralty, re-
gretting that no use could be found for my services.
This was stupefying. Fingering the Admiralty's letter,
I noticed the printer's reference number on the bottom at
the end. I had worked in Government offices of various
types for years, and a thought struck me. I picked up a
pen and wrote back to say that I had received their Lord-
ships' communication, but had noticed that it was on a
standard printed form; was it possible that the clerk
engaged in dealing with the applications had pulled a
form by mistake from the wrong pile?

This piece of expertise produced the offer of a commission by return of post, and I had rushed off to Brighton
before this second communication could be recalled.

It is odd to consider how extremely little a man in the
ordinary world—even a yachtsman—knew about naval
life. I had shot rabbits and shot at birds for years, but
knew nothing about explosives. I had dined frequently
with my naval brother in the barracks at Portsmouth,
but had never considered distinctions of rank, or supposed
that anybody under the level of an Admiral was a person
of much consequence. I had never bled so much as a
pint. Entering *King Alfred*, mercifully in civilian clothes,
I reported to the officer-in-charge and was told to find

my "class captain"; I should have no difficulty, as he would be wearing a D.S.O.

I realized with a shock that I had not the faintest notion what a D.S.O. ribbon looked like. In this place, it appeared that a Lieutenant-Commander was a high functionary. A Captain was a God. I had been in the building hardly half an hour when an appalling explosion shook the place and I flung myself down in the passage. It turned out to be nothing but a practice blank shot from the *King Alfred* six-inch gun, mounted outside on the tarmac.

The first lecture was on the "hour angle of the mean sun", a conception, apparently, of value in navigation.

The naval chapters in this book are not intended to contain digressions but no one, I think, who has read and enjoyed Sir Osbert Sitwell's exquisite autobiography could consider a book to be a book at all which did not contain, or indeed really consist of them. I will, therefore, at once remark that we were all, of course, whether ratings or officers, playing at being sailors, an attitude which I believe always puzzled the regular naval officers, and even troubled them, for they knew, as by instinct, that the basis of normal discipline was by that fact cut away, and they hesitated to accept whole-heartedly the alternative which we offered to them, an obedience resting in part upon respect for such special experience as they possessed, and in part upon a deliberate intention to play the game, for the duration of the war, according to the rules as far as we could discern them. In this case, illusions had been preserved as far as possible, and the ratings did live upon a lower deck, in so far as their sleeping quarters were confined to the cellars and the basement. They accepted their curious garments, their little hard round hats, their bibs, their skimpy blouses and billowy trousers, with philosophic humour. We officers eyed these extraordinary relics of a past age with cautious curiosity wondering whether we could decently ask how they were put on and what, if anything, lay below the outer surfaces. Later, in the Fleet at large, as the ranks were flooded with civilians, the R.N.V.R. officers found themselves appointed by the lower deck as informal "political commissars", successors to the chaplains, intermediaries between the ratings and the old regular naval officers, who were treated with indulgence by the sailors in view of the serious business in hand but occasionally passed all bearing and then we would be asked to intervene. "Tell the old B—" we would be asked, "that if he does that again we shall throw him into the sea."

Five weeks went by in the process of acquiring some familiarity with these categories of thought. Men passed through the centre with bewildering rapidity, being pulled out at a moment's notice for various assignments for which they either were, or were not, suited. I was by then myself a class captain and had just paraded my squad for a period of drill outside in the yard when a secret signal was brought up by an orderly. The first heavy air raid on London had taken place the night before.

The signal stated that twelve volunteers were required from the Fleet to attempt to dismantle a number of German magnetic mines which had been dropped on London by parachute. (These were the great mines which the public at once, though not really correctly, named "land mines".)

I read the signal out to my squad and asked any volunteers to take one pace forward. The entire squad of thirty moved a pace nearer. I dismissed the party and dashed to the Commanding Officer, hoping to reach his office before he had taken all the names he needed. I reported that all my squad wished to go, but pleaded that I, as class captain, might be allowed preference. I was handed a railway warrant and told to go immediately to H.M.S. *Vernon*, the headquarters of the Torpedo and Mining Department in Portsmouth.

CHAPTER TWO

RUGBY
1921

"Sequor autem, si quomodo comprehendam"
Philipp. 3

In the train for Portsmouth, as we slipped along in the September sunshine below Arundel Castle, it was borne in on me that I could hardly have much longer to live.

Life till then had not been tranquil. It had contained a series of adventures; the course had been poignant and sometimes tiring. Saint Teresa (of Spain, not of Lisieux) divides religion into two kinds; there are those who have to draw their water for themselves in buckets from a well, and those who have it poured from above them on to their heads. I had always been in the second class, but though in rare intervals I had had time to long for tranquillity, and in rarer intervals still had even experienced it, it had always seemed clear that I must live my life in the rough and tumble.

Religion in England in the second quarter of the twentieth century must have been less understood than at any period since the Egyptians erected the Pyramids. Members of the Student Christian Movement and its surroundings were fond of saying before the war that religion must be caught, not taught. It is arguable that religion now affects so few that the majority, if they are to have any religion, must learn it; they can hardly hope to catch it.

For my own part, I had had the good fortune to have been brought up in a house where each day began with prayers. They followed a ritual originally written for the family by John Keble. Our own methods were a compromise between two schools of thought and practice. My mother's family had always been *novi homines*. One had been a man of the Reformation and a member of the Privy Council in each of the three Protestant Tudor reigns, the gaoler of Mary Queen of Scots at Fotheringay. Nothing now remains of his castle by the bridge over the Nene except an enormous block of rubble from the keep, rolled by an explosion down to the reedy edge of the river below and now confined behind a rusty iron railing; but his helmet, lance and iron gloves still hang on the wall above the ornamental tomb in his church at Standon in Hertfordshire. Another member of the family, in the nineteenth century, had been Member of Parliament for Ashton-under-Lyme and the ally of Lord Shaftesbury and Richard Oastler in the movement to improve the conditions of the poorer classes. My grandmother in Yorkshire rented a pew in the Parish Church for the morning service and another in the Methodist Chapel for the afternoon. Her eldest son, Sir Michael Sadler, became Vice-Chancellor of Leeds University. At prayers in the Sadler house in

London the family sat in easy chairs round the room: my grandmother would read a chapter from the Scriptures, and then, as she began the Lord's Prayer, we would turn and kneel into our chairs, presenting our backs to the rest of the assembly. The chairs were old, large and comfortable, upholstered in a faded brown. In the ordinary day-time hours, dotted about the room and deprived of their kneeling occupants, they seemed like desolate elephants. My father's family, on the other hand, represented the old land-owning tradition of the West Country—high and dry Church, crossed, some way back, with Scottish Quakerism. At my grandmother's house at Cheddon Fitzpaine in Somerset, morning prayers were a stately occasion. They were held in the "morning room", a long sunny room facing south. The east wall was covered with a curtain, behind which was a large crucifix suspended upon a violet backcloth. Before breakfast, a gong was sounded; the family would file in, followed by the servants, and kneel upon the carpet in five or six rows, one behind the other arranged in strict order of precedence. After a short pause, the eldest of the sons in residence (whether in Holy Orders or not) would enter, draw the curtain back, and proceed in a reverent manner to read the Keble litanies.

There was always a sense of distinction between the upper and the lower classes and a certain licence was of necessity allowed to the former. Take for instance, the case of croquet. The house was in essence a mere façade; its rooms, yards and stables and the high walls of the

fruit garden formed a frame for a croquet lawn, a great
stretch of grass always kept in perfect condition. In
summer the sunny hours were compounded of the noise
of bees and pigeons, of cutters in the cornfields, the
distant soft explosion of shot guns and from behind the
house the click of croquet mallets on the balls. The
mallets lived in wooden boxes in a potting shed: in a
second box was kept a special set of mallets with circles
cut from the rubber soles of cricket boots, nailed to the
striking faces. These numbing circles made any real
croquet impossible, but a game of a sort could be played
with them. These mallets were for use on Sunday after-
noons. It would not be right it was thought, that the
well-known sounds should be allowed officially to apprise
the villagers that croquet was being played as usual on
the Manor House lawn on a Sunday afternoon, still more
on a Sunday morning. True, these things could not be
hid and the villagers must inevitably know but at least
a gesture had been made and anyone who knew anything at all about croquet must realize what an agonizing
penance the family had imposed upon themselves in
honour of the Lord's Day by insisting upon using such
atrocious blunted instruments. On these days, therefore,
an almost absolute silence on the lawn was broken only
by the clanging of the bells from the church over the
wall, ringing with an angular crescendo, and uneven,
quickening tempo, to the ritual climax five minutes
before the service was due to begin; when the balloon
of noise collapsed, to be succeeded by the soft tolling of

a single bell and my father and his brothers hastily kicked off their rubber-soled croquet shoes, carefully replaced the mallets in the box, recalled their minds to their religious duties and walked with a gentle dignity into the nave, the eldest disappearing into the vestry, where he could be seen through the open door struggling with his outstretched arms into a large white surplice like some enormous black and white scarecrow.

It was natural that these contrasts should produce in the grandchildren something of a crossbench mind in matters of religion; and, perhaps, that we should have come to the conclusion, having tried both, that we preferred a trace of ritualism to the more Protestant forms of worship.

However, it was at Rugby School in 1921, at the age of eighteen, that it first struck me that life as lived in England by the well-to-do classes appeared to have acquired an element of unreality. It was not the political, the economic or the religious unreality which struck home first, but the unreality in people's personal lives. There was a master on the staff named "Napoleon" Smith. Both he and his wife were painters, and they lived, remote from footballs and the general desolation, in an upstairs flat in the Barby Road. Smith never intentionally "unsettled" a boy but if asked for his advice, he would occasionally throw out a suggestion. He proposed that I should have a look at Freud's *Interpretation of Dreams*.

Rather alarmed, I asked my headmaster, Dr. David (subsequently Bishop of Saint Edmundsbury, and Liverpool) whether he would sanction this. He consented, making one condition—that I should come and tell him what I thought of the book when I had finished it. I borrowed an English translation from Boots' library.

To me the book appeared to be dealing with real things, however difficult might be the language and the approach; and I was horrified to discover that the general run of my elders would have nothing to do with it. They appeared to prefer to continue to live in what seemed to be a series of conventional responses, without asking what were really the springs of action. My uncle Sadler used to say that his definition of religion was "facing the facts". I never could understand why so large a section of the English upper classes so steadfastly refused to acknowledge the facts in the ordinary way of life and behaviour.

CHAPTER THREE

THE ADMIRALTY FROM INSIDE

"Significavit Deus quae oportet fieri cito."
Apoc. 1

The train ran into Portsmouth towards evening. The *Vernon* consisted of an area of the Dockyard cut up with quays and basins and carrying a great variety of buildings—an officers' mess, which looked as if it had been built in the days of King Edward VII, tall old warehouses in eighteenth-century brick and a number of iron sheds, some fitted up as workshops, some as stores and some as instructional schools. We were told that we should be there for forty-eight hours for some preliminary instruction in the principles of mine design, and after that we would report to the Admiralty.

In one shed was an actual specimen of an early design of German magnetic mine from the current war. It had been brought in from the shallows of the Thames estuary a year earlier by Lieut.-Commander Ouvry, D.S.O. A certain humour attached to that incident: Ouvry had succeeded in tracing and removing a fuse, assumed that the mine was then reasonably safe and had had it hoisted into a lorry and driven in to the *Vernon*; it was taken entirely to pieces there and a second complete detonating system was discovered.

We eyed this mine with some apprehension. All the elements had been cleaned and polished in naval fashion and then put together again, and the whole monstrous machine was lying like a great dull green cigar, ten feet long, on a big steel tray, and with a touch of the hand we could turn any part of the mine up into a convenient position for examination. Ouvry himself walked in and pointed out one or two items in his quiet way. He was still speaking when suddenly the sirens sounded and to our astonishment everybody packed up and made for the shelters. In September, 1940, all Admiralty establishments were still working to rule. The extraordinary thing was that from that moment on, Portsmouth was under continual warning and we saw no more of the mine or the shed. We did gather, however, that we were expected to open these mines up and take out what we should find inside the carcase. If we noticed anything like the fuse Ouvry had pointed out, we had better start with that. We might find it in the nose. We were introduced to a few tools and shown their uses.

When our forty-eight hours were up, we were ordered to leave by the afternoon train for London. We politely pointed out that we had really received very little instruction and could hardly regard ourselves as qualified to tackle a live mine. This submission was waved aside, with the remark that we need not take things too seriously; we should be going out in the first instance with an expert.

We reached the Admiralty at six o'clock and were

directed upstairs to a room on the third floor overlooking Whitehall. We threaded our way through the dirty passages and went up in a lift. Standing in the middle of the room was a white-haired naval Captain with a sheaf of papers under his arm. We had no time to observe more than a massive clean-shaven face, the four golden rings on his sleeve and a singularly honourable and piercing pair of eyes.

Sweeping us into a half-circle he proceeded to deal out his papers, about twenty sheets to each man. I looked quickly at mine and saw that each sheet carried an address, a date and a time. "When you have dealt with those," said the Captain, "you can come back and let me know."

We exchanged anxious glances. "But who is taking us, sir?" I asked. "TAKING YOU," said the Captain, "You're taking yourselves. Get out! But before you go, pick up a set of tools from the table, and choose a sailor from that row over there against the wall. You will find a line of service cars outside in Spring Gardens; take which you like of those." We turned and saw a line of twelve sailors slouched against the partition. I had certainly never seen such a villainous set of men in my existence. Each carried what appeared to be sergeant's stripes in red upon his arm. As my eye passed along the line of faces every jaw was moving slowly—every man was chewing a quid of tobacco. All, except one. As the senior man, I had to speak first. There was no time to hang about, so in desperation I chose—I chose the only motion-less jaw. It belonged to Able Seaman Stephen Tuckwell.

It turned out that he was the finest fellow who ever put in eighteen years' service with the Royal Navy.

The tools were contained in long wooden boxes, rather like the croquet boxes at my grandmother's house in Somerset. They included spanners of various sorts and sizes, and other special gadgets, all made, by the *Vernon* workshops, in non-magnetic materials. A mysterious item was a child's wooden spade; but of that later. The whole outfit was surprisingly heavy. Our sailors grabbed the boxes, and we went downstairs to look for a car. We were each to make for a spot thought to be most convenient as a headquarters from which to start on our assignment with the first light of the following day.

We stumbled out into Spring Gardens. There wasn't a car in sight. A little bewildered we returned to the Captain's room. "Oh, no cars," said he. "I'm not surprised. Naval Stores." Without hesitation he picked up his telephone and asked for the War Office. When the girl answered, the Captain said "Admiralty speaking; give me the top General in Transport." This personage was duly connected. The Captain explained the nature and urgency of our work; could the War Office possibly supply twelve large cars at once? "Certainly," said the General. Twelve large Humbers came round immediately, and from that day onwards the entire transport of the section, including drivers, was supplied, free of charge, by the Army. In course of time, they assigned us a complete R.A.S.C. Company.

Settled in my Humber, I began looking more carefully

through my sheaf of addresses. I saw to my delight that my "parish" was the area lying between the Thames and King's Lynn. A heavy proportion of the mines were down in Essex and my headquarters was to be Great Dunmow. At Thaxted, at Lady Warwick's house at Great Easton a few miles away, and again at Burnham Overy Staithe near Lynn, some of my greatest spiritual adventures hitherto had taken place. It seemed that this phase of life, or what remained of it was to form an integral part of what had gone before. Anyhow, I knew the way.

CHAPTER FOUR

OXFORD
1922-24

*"Quemadmodum cervus ad fontes aquarum, ita desiderat
anima mea ad te, Deus".*
Ps. 41

I remember the profound excitement with which I
first saw the spires of Oxford, in the autumn of 1922.
I saw them, as many must, from a Great Western
Railway train on the line from London through Didcot.
They were gleaming, a pale golden colour, against a
curtain of grey mist.

It was at Oxford that life first began to run away from
me. The difficulty was that none of the so to say "official"
guides seemed to be really interested in the questions
with which I was concerned. But it was intensely
exciting to be free to give my whole self to the search for
the answers.

My first act was to get hold of Jung's *Psychological
Types*. Meanwhile, I was given a good deal too much
to read in the way of classical literature. As far as I can
recall, the first of the two parts of the classical school then
required the undergraduate to read the whole of the works
of Virgil, Cicero, Homer and Demosthenes. The
amount of Greek I read in those two years permanently

affected my eyesight. I read it, though reluctantly, and must in the process have absorbed, if only half consciously, some of the thought and some of the beauty. There are disadvantages, in the modern day, in having acquired a sense of perfection; but I was not aware of it then, and there were even at the time compensating advantages.

At Rugby, where as in Parliament and in some big business, the classical tradition ruled supreme, I had been driven to suppose that nobody in authority was likely to take great interest in the nature of reality and at Oxford it did not, unfortunately, occur to me that I might find help among the scientific or medical staff. I pursued the track through books alone; I walked with Havelock Ellis over the dome of St. Paul's; and thus acquired an impression which later experience has never wholly removed that convention was the death of the soul and the "left" the only possible framework for a life of the mind.

In the cold weather I spent many hours roaming over Cumnor Hill, looking out over Ferry Hinksey and thinking, wisps of white steam from the railway drifting below across the spires and the valley of the Cherwell, green in the rain and grey-white in the snow: in summer I would stroke a punt to some sunny backwater on the river, tie up to a branch and read.

In the spring of 1924, C. R. Cruttwell, then Dean and later Principal of my college, took me with him for a a holiday in the south of France. His reason for doing so, he said, was that it had been reported to him that I was the only undergraduate in the building who could render Virgil into reasonable English! Anyhow, we went to Dijon, Avignon, Les Baux, Nîmes, Arles, the Pont du Gard, the eastern end of the Pyrénées, Carcassonne and Toulouse. It was perhaps primarily a wine-tasting expedition and the wines we tasted were as glorious as could be found anywhere. But for me, to whom everything was so new, the sights were as entrancing as the tastes.

My uncle Sadler, then Master of University College, had lent me Vincent van Gogh's "Olive Garden"—the original. It was one of the truly enormous collection of modern paintings which he kept in his house. Constant, almost daily wanderings through those rooms had steeped my mind in the work of Constable, Wilson Steer, Cézanne, van Gogh, Matisse, Renoir, Segonzac, Manet, Duncan Grant, Sisley and Monet—to name those only who were perhaps my favourites. The collection was far too large to display, even in a big house. He kept the bulk of it stacked tightly face to face in racks in the billiards-room and the attics. Later, at Headington, he took to collecting statuary; the stuff overflowed into the garden, and one might be startled, at the Rookery, by figures of bizarre shape, at the end of any vista, or behind any clump of bushes.

His method, in the house, was to ring the changes, banishing perhaps fifty or sixty pictures to the racks and bringing out others. That did not matter so much to one like myself who was privileged to have access to the house on any day and even to visit the racks; but I did much dislike his habit of selling particular treasures of mine(!) in order to buy something of later date, or, as often happened, to help painters who were in temporary need of cash, or encouragement. He liked—and with reason—to back his own judgment.[1]

The pictures threw an astonishing light upon the countryside of France when I came to see it. But not only upon France. After some hours' study of the paintings, any ordinary English scene took on an entirely different aspect. I had always passionately loved the English countryside, but it was the French painters, particularly Monet, who showed me a new way to look at it. Indeed, the pictures played a very large part in that steady process by which, during my last year at Rugby and my whole time at Oxford, I was being taken away from the ordinary world.

One afternoon in the Pyrénées Cruttwell and I walked up a track into the mountains above the gorge of Axat. We decided to take a short cut back, down a promising looking cleft in the hillside. All went well till we got down to about five hundred feet from the bottom, when we found ourselves at the top of a precipitous drop of about fifteen feet above what seemed to be the final scree leading to the open valley. We took the admitted risk of letting ourselves go over this precipitous drop, and

[1] For what to me is a delightful and convincing portrait of my uncle Sadler, I would refer readers to his son's memoir: *Michael Ernest Sadler* by Michael Sadleir, London, 1949.

found to our horror that we were trapped. The scree ended in a sheer cliff: the sides of the gully could nowhere be climbed, and the little precipice behind us was unscalable. We stood at the top of the cliff, "treading water", as it were, in the loose stones of the scree, which poured over with a steady rattle below us. The floor of the gully was so steep that it was impossible even to find a place flat enough to sit down and rest. The only thing beside the sky to be seen from where we were was a blank mountainside across the gorge, which was obviously hardly ever visited. A few vultures sailed quietly overhead.

Darkness was falling and with the last light we hooked ourselves round the stem of a bush at the side of the gully, wrapped our thighs, under our trousers, with sheets of the *Continental Daily Mail* which I had fortunately stuffed into my pocket in the hotel before leaving, and went to sleep. We had no food or drink; it was exceedingly cold; and we were both convinced that we should have to die where we lay. Neither of us made any remarks. An occasional train hooted and clattered through a tunnel on the other side of the gorge.

With the first light, we made a further reconnaissance of the sides of the gully. At this second attempt, I found I could just scramble out from the top of a small fir-tree which was growing against the rock, and give Cruttwell, who was much larger and heavier than myself, the necessary help to follow me.

As we sat, panting, on the open ground, Cruttwell

offered only one comment. In his curious gruff, staccato grunt he remarked, "Thank God, you didn't pray."

I should have been even more delighted than I was at this astonishing piece of inconsistency on the part of the well-known historian. I had not prayed for the very good reason that I did not suppose that there was anyone to whom prayers could usefully be addressed. In one of the psychological books I had read, I had come across the suggestion that God was a "hypostatized abstraction" and for the time being I was quite content to leave it at that.

The experience at Axat threw a strange light upon the securities of ordinary existence: it appeared that one could leave a station hotel at three o'clock on a Saturday afternoon, and be as good as dead by nightfall. This sort of thing happened in detective stories, it was true, but then people in detective stories were either criminals or detectives, and laid themselves open to it—or if they were merely the members of the house-party, they were usually only dummies and in any case were the victims of authors.

Looking back over those first two years at Oxford I am painfully aware of how little apparent use I made of them. And yet in my defence I would plead that those who would condemn me, if only as a type of under-graduate, should consider the point from which I started. It can surely never have been easy for a young man trained in the classical side of a public school of the early part of this century to find for himself a clue to

34

reality. My mother's family had few illusions, great aesthetic gifts and an extraordinary power of initiative but, curiously enough, it was my father's family which had the dominant influence upon my mind. This was due to a variety of causes, perhaps basically to the combination of great strength and sweetness in their moral character, and to the fascination of the long tradition of political control which my forebears on my father's side had exercised right back beyond historical record. Only in Stuart times had they themselves occupied high places since the Reformation, but from pre-Reformation times they inherited the arms of a large number of the families represented on the roll of those who accompanied the Conqueror in his enterprise and though throughout the eighteenth and nineteenth centuries they had generally been merely country squires, two or three hundred years is not a long time in the history of a family and behind the true benevolence of their customs they retained, clearly enough, the knowledge that their position and that of the entire governing class rested originally upon that long-ago Norman conquest; the view was that the "new men" of the Reformation had not created a new society —they had extorted certain modifications in the framework but when they had modified it they had accepted it and had indeed been accepted into it. The Sadlers, therefore, though almost infinitely more brilliant than my father's family, seemed really to represent no more than the gadfly element in society, and when it came down to who was landlord and who was tenant and who should ultimately control the distribution of real assets, their activities, it seemed, could still in the last resort, be brushed aside. It is, I think, not untrue to say that until the very end of the eighteenth century the conditions which were ultimately to bring about a socialistic order of society, for a time at any rate, never existed. It was not until the vast growth of population, concentrated in towns, both helped to create the possibility of mass production and in turn made society dependent for defence and even for existence upon its continuance, that persuasion came to assume its important place in English politics. Dictatorship, whether called Fascist, Bolshevist or merely Plantagenet or Hanoverian, can maintain the output of factories but it requires the authorities to go to very great lengths, to construct concentration camps and gas chambers and the rest which are distasteful at times even to themselves. I think my father's family in common with the majority of the English gentry, had not realized precisely what line the manufacturers, under pressure of circumstances, had decided for the time being to take. They were not a party to the experiment in persuasion; living on the wings, as it were, in their manor houses in the country, which death duties had not yet stripped from them, they had, in general, not grasped the change in the economic balance of society; they had not been consulted, they had not even asked to be informed, they merely retained a knowledge that force had been applied with success in the past and was indeed the normal mechanism of control, requiring as it did close genuine ties between the commander and only a comparatively small number of troops, call them at various times storm troopers, police, beadles or what you will.

Thus, I and my contemporaries in the university from the public schools, apart from a few of the sons of great industrialists, were absolutely ignorant of the part we should be asked to play. I would say that this is the fundamental criticism which must be levelled at the public schools of the time and no argument can be advanced to excuse them; unless it be that schools cannot be expected to deal in anything short of long-term policy, and that force must in the end return, if only because the mass of the people are unlikely to be able to see that their very existence depends upon the brains and initiative of others, and will therefore persist to their own ruin, in taking their present conditions for granted. Added then to this ignorance of the sources of our bread and butter which I shared with my friends, I brought with me from Rugby only the first beginnings of an appreciation of beauty in the arts, no knowledge of science and the most primitive of religious equipment.

The first I owed, granted the foundation in myself of a love of landscape which can only be called passionate, to Napoleon Smith and the Rev. H. H. Symonds, later Headmaster of the Liverpool Institute but in the early 'twenties, fortunately for us, the master in charge of the classical upper sixth at Rugby. Looking back, it is difficult to calculate how much we owed to H. H. Symonds; his scholarship must have been of a high order, but his mind was not purely literary in character and he overflowed beyond the normal curriculum of Latin and Greek verse and prose (though exacting from us in these respects the uttermost farthing) in three directions at least—into Greek and Latin art, socialism and psychology and I certainly owe to his lectures on Greek sculpture the only "alpha" mark I ever obtained in an Oxford examination. Further, though I have ascribed my original liberation to Napoleon Smith I must owe something to Symonds in psychology; also in politics, for it was he who compelled us to read Ruskin's *Fors Clavigera* and *Unto This Last* and though we considered these writings eccentric at the time the fascination of the style must have deposited the thought a damaging distance inside our ramparts.

At school I had been allowed to learn science for no more than three weeks. In those three lessons we had carried out an elementary titration, purely by rule of thumb, and in physics we had gone so far as to hang weights upon a wire until the point was reached at which the wire suddenly stretched and parted and the weights fell upon a piece of doormat. I had no conception of the atomic or any other scientific theory and I could not even have made a list of the main organs of my own body.

At Oxford it was then natural, though it was certainly greatly to be deplored, that I should find my compass needle swinging rather violently as I cast about for the right course. Plunged into a much larger and richer world, it was difficult to tell at first where lay the line of advance and where I might best begin to discover how the world worked and what I should do in it. A certain facility with language had unfortunately been taken at school as a reason for putting me on the classical side and I had been imprisoned from the age of fourteen onwards in an impossibly narrow curriculum. Theoretically, I should immediately have concentrated upon my classics at Oxford also; but I must have felt instinctively that that would have been a fatal decision and I made up my mind to have no more to do with Greek and Latin than was absolutely necessary. Much as I owe to the French painters, they undoubtedly arrested a great part of my attention in those two years: armed with the criticism of Roger Fry and Clive Bell, I tried hard to understand the meaning of their interpretation of the world, which was certainly quite independent of the doctrines of Dr. Arnold, and seemed to point the way to some separate grasp of what was significant.

Had some of this general background been filled in for me in earlier years I might have pursued reality further in Paris, or in St. Petersburg, or in the Foreign Legion, or in Tibet; as it was I sat in Oxford and struggled by myself from one book to another.

CHAPTER FIVE

A MINE AT BRENTWOOD

"Exeamus igitur ad eum extra castra"
Hebr. 13

The nearest address on Captain Currey's list was at Brentwood, so I decided to spend the first night in London and see what this mine looked like on my way into Essex in the morning.

We had discovered at Hove and at Portsmouth that the basic principle of any mine was the detonation of an explosive charge by means of an electrical current. There are two main classes of mine, the contact and the non-contact, that is, mines which are designed to float and only blow up if a ship rams them, and mines which are laid on the bottom of the sea and are set off from a distance. The first type is in essence a large hollow metal football, measuring generally about three feet across at most, the inside partly packed with explosive material, usually in the shape of a great number of small slabs, enough (empty) air space being left to ensure that the whole contraption will float in water. The operative feature is the horn of the mine. These horns, made of soft metal like brass or lead, contain a glass bottle of electrolyte. When the mine strikes the side of a ship, the horns bend sideways, the glass bottles break and the electrolyte runs down a tube into a prepared battery which it activates. The result is an electric current which passes through, and by that process heats up, a wire which is bedded in a small packet of explosive of a type specially sensitive to temperature, known to the profession as a "puffer".

There is, in practice, a fairly severe limit to the size of a floating mine; the ball must contain not merely the explosive charge but also enough empty space to cause it to float, and if it is to contain more than a certain amount of explosive, say 200 to 300 pounds, the carcase has to be so large that it becomes impossible to handle in a minelayer. Minelayers must be fairly small if they are to be manoeuvred in the comparatively restricted approaches to harbours where mines are usually laid.

The mine is attached by a cable to a heavy block of metal which acts as an anchor; the cable is set to a length which will ensure that the mine floats out of sight a few feet below the surface of the water. To "sweep" these mines, in the ordinary way, you drag a stout cable, fitted with heavy wire-cutting equipment, between two ships for example; the cable cuts the mine cables, the mines bob up to the top and from a safe distance away on the surface you give them a burst of machine-gun fire in the horns. By international practice a contact mine must be so designed that if it parts from its cable the current cannot flow through the puffer, and in theory a mine found floating loose, or washed up on a beach is safe to handle. But it will be understood that it is risky to assume that this will be so.

The non-contact mine, on the other hand, is designed not to float but to lie on the bed of a channel. It is much heavier, usually weighing at least a ton and can be operated by a variety of processes. For instance, it can be linked with the shore by an electric cable and detonated when required by a man on the look-out who has simply to press a contact key. Other types can be detonated by the noise of a ship's engines and propellers overhead (the "acoustic" mine), or by the concentration in the earth's natural magnetic field which is caused by the passage overhead of a ship's heavy mass of metal. This concentration is sufficient to deflect a compass needle, the end of which can be arranged to make contact with a pin connected to a battery and so complete an electrical circuit through a "puffer". The type of magnetic pressure required to move the needles used need not exceed a few thousandths of an ounce.

In dealing with a magnetic or even an acoustic mine, therefore, we were dealing in any case with an exceedingly sensitive instrument. But that was not all, for the mines contained a self-destruction device in the nose, designed to set them off if they received the least shock. This was by origin a precaution but it became the reason why these huge weapons came to be used as bombs on cities. A small clockwork fuse formed part of the mechanism. The mines were usually dropped on parachutes from low-flying aircraft. The fuse was designed to start with the shock administered when the mine hit the surface of the water. A subsidiary arrangement checked the clock if the mine did in fact fall into as much as twenty or thirty feet of water, i.e. into a port channel; if the mine were aimed badly or blown by the wind to one side so that it fell into shallow water, or on to dry land where there would be some prospect of examining it, this subsidiary device was not brought into operation and in the ordinary course of events the mine blew up and destroyed itself. The Germans determined to take advantage of this to use the mines as bombs knowing that if they fell anywhere on land they would almost instantly blow up and cause enormous damage. It will be seen, if this explanation has been sufficiently clear, that an unexploded magnetic mine on land was in itself something of an anomaly. The obvious conclusion was either that the mine had been deliberately set for delayed action, or that it had suffered some damage in its fall and in that case the problem was, what was the nature of the damage, and exactly how dangerous was the condition of the weapon. In practice, we found that the fuse could be set going by the least vibration, for instance the vibration caused by a lorry passing in the street, or a tube train moving below in a tunnel. The time of its run before detonation was normally less than half a minute. If it started while one was working on the mine, one might or might not, have as much as twenty-two seconds in which to escape; it depended upon whether the clock had already travelled a part of its run and had merely stuck for some mechanical reason or other—poor manufacture, or perhaps damage. These clocks frequently started, and the question then was whether to down tools and run at once, or to try to get the fuse right out before it detonated. A minor difficulty was that if one could withdraw the fuse from the main primer before it fired (which would save the mine itself) one might still be left with the subsidiary primer in position on the fuse, in which case one might be killed, lose a hand or be blinded.

It will be understood then, that in general terms our problem was first to remove the clockwork fuse and then, before carrying out any other investigations to find and break any circuits leading to "puffers"; setting about the work in such a way as not, if possible, to operate the main detonating system or systems. As an illustration of the interest of the subject it might be mentioned that these magnetic mines contained a mechanism which set them automatically for latitude, the strength of the earth's magnetic field varying, as it does, between the poles of the equator. But this is in part anticipation.

Well, I always enjoyed breakfast and it was only after a good one (still obtainable then) that I drove out to the Air Raid Precautions Headquarters in Brentwood, and asked for directions. The A.R.P. Officer was there, and also His Worship the Mayor, and both kindly insisted on conducting me personally to the site. I was to leave my car outside the office and go in theirs.

On the tarmac was a large Daimler, with a big notice in black and white hung over the radiator—"AMBU-LANCE". It became clear that we were to get into this ill-omened vehicle. I expected to be killed, or at least seriously wounded and I could not understand why that possibility had not occurred to them. To put me straight into an ambulance, while still alive, seemed the best possible way to destroy what nerve I could still summon up.

I was later to discover that on this mining assignment the worse the omens were, the better the luck. No clearer example could be quoted than the case of the Cardiff Municipal Mortuary. But I will tell that story later.

I had never seen an explosion of any kind at this stage, I had no idea of the effect of the detonation of even half a ton of explosive, and was quite unaware that if a mine went up while I was working on it, there would be nothing whatever left of me. It was, as a matter of fact, one of the pleasanter things about life in our party that for a long time we never had to have a funeral, because if an accident happened, there was never anything left to bury; not even a cigarette case.

This particular mine was down in the middle of a wood and we left the car and started walking down a track. The wood was quite small, we walked quite a way, and I began to get nervous. I asked the Mayor whether he had not better stay where he was and let me go on alone. "Oh, no," he said, "there is no need to be

45

anxious—we haven't yet got to the constable." They had apparently stationed a constable to keep off intruders. I relapsed into silence and we went on walking.

I was opening my mouth to protest again, when we rounded a corner to the left and there, in a small clearing, stood a constable in uniform and within a foot of his legs was a curious object like a very large green saucepan.

I drew an involuntary breath. The saucepan was nothing but the hollow end of the mine, which in the ordinary way contains the parachute; the parachute was nowhere to be seen, and the mine itself was buried with its nose nine feet down in the gravel.

Being always weak in imagination, I had somehow not conceived to myself that I should ever find a mine in such a position. If I had not actually assumed that they would all have been carefully cleaned by the sailors at Portsmouth and laid out on a tray so that I could get at them easily, I had at least vaguely supposed that they would all be lying out lengthways on the ground with the important parts upwards. That one could be completely buried had never entered my head.

I stood and contemplated the horrible saucepan with the Mayor on one side and the A.R.P. officer on the other. Glancing helplessly around, the thing we were always told not to do in the classrooms at Rugby, I noticed that the trees were young and the mine had smashed off some of the branches as it fell. I suddenly realized the probable function of the wooden spade in my tool kit;

the idea probably was that I should dig down, alone, nine feet through the gravel to the fuse in the nose, shifting each spadeful with the greatest care.

I was not left long to these reflections. "Well, sir," began the Mayor, "What do you think of *that*?" "Well, sir," I replied with what craft I could summon, "I think that is the most interesting case I have ever seen." I was rather pleased to be able to put it that way, which was indeed the truth because I had never been called upon at any time before to contemplate a live magnetic mine in a way of business.

"Well, sir," continued the Mayor, "*what are you going to do about it?*"

This question roused me to action. I was, after all, supposed to be an Admiralty expert, I was dressed in naval uniform, and on no account could I allow civilians to suspect that I had not the least idea what the mine contained or how I should tackle it. I pulled from my pocket the sheaf of addresses given me by Captain Currey and waved it in his face. "I am going to do *nothing*, Mr. Mayor," I answered.

"*Nothing?*" said he, "but surely that is not possible?"

"*Nothing*," I said firmly, "I have a list here of more than twenty mines of high priority; many are lying in important buildings like telephone exchanges and power stations. This thing is lying in a wood. If it goes up to-morrow, it won't do any damage. I shall come back in a fortnight."

I left them at the A.R.P. office, bolted round the

corner into the main street, into the first telephone box, and rang up the Captain.

I explained that the mine was buried to the tail in a wood and asked him what I was to do.

"*DO?*" shouted the Captain down the telephone, "*DO? Blow it up: you bloody fool*" and he slammed down the receiver.

I had never blown up anything in my life and I had not the slightest idea how to set about it. To attempt anything of the sort in this case seemed anyhow exceedingly dangerous. I went down to the Police Station and asked whether there was an Army Bomb Squad working in the district. "Why, yes, sir," said the sergeant, "there's Captain Shelburne, down by the mill."

I drove down to the mill and there, sure enough, was Captain Shelburne. A very gallant comrade-in-arms he proved to be for many months after this. Assuming an air of detachment, for the sake of appearances, I remarked that I had a big magnetic mine down in a wood the other side of the town: would it by any chance amuse his men to blow it up?

The Captain leant over the edge of a large hole, the sides shored up with timber, and apparently going down indefinitely into the earth, like the sides of a lift shaft in a tube station. "Tom!" he yelled. There was an answering call and the Captain explained the situation. Covered with clay, the sergeant came up and in a few moments a party was climbing into the Bomb Squad van, with a small coil of what looked like rubber-covered wire, a

48

few slabs of stuff that resembled coarse wall-board, about the size of a big pocket note-book, some night-lights (?), and some little red tin pencils, about an inch and a half long. We drove to the wood, turned straight down the track without a moment's hesitation and took the car right into the clearing. Whistling and smoking they dug round the top end of the mine, not apparently in the least worried about the effect upon its health, set the guncotton slabs against one side, fitted the primers and detonators, put about eighteen inches of the Bickford's fuse on each, lit the ends with a match and advised a rapid departure.

There was a heavy explosion, and when we came back we found a crater in the gravel about twenty feet across. Over a drink, I begged some of the Army demolition outfit. The Captain gave me enough to last for a fort-night.

—————

CHAPTER SIX

OXFORD
1925

Tunc dixi, "Ecce venio"
Ps. 39

On my return from the Pyrénées, the pace at
Oxford quickened sharply. The second part
of the classical course consisted of two subjects,
the history of the ancient empires of Greece and Rome,
and their art and philosophy. Two books only were set
for the philosophical part of the examination, Plato's
Republic and Aristotle's *Ethics*—both in the original
Greek—but we were expected also to answer questions
about later developments in thought about ethics, logic,
the theory of perception, the nature of reality and of the
human mind and the relations between the one and the
other. In my time, standard books were those of Des-
cartes, Locke, Berkeley and Hume and among more
modern writers, T. H. Green, F. H. Bradley and Bosan-
quet. The last two had the most direct bearing upon the
subjects which interested me.

On the shelves of the library in Hertford College there
were two small books, one in the brown cloth binding
of the Home University Library and the other in faded
dark blue.

The first was *Some Problems of Philosophy* by Bertrand Russell. This book provided my first explicit introduction to the fact that it is impossible to state precisely what colour any object really is. Russell points out that if an object is looked at carefully, it becomes clear that the colour is much affected at all places on the surface by light or shadow reflected from things around it, and everything actually carries a great number of quite different colours. For some reason I had not clearly recognized this before, although I had spent so much time with the French pictures at my uncle's house, I had given myself over more to their atmosphere and to their interpretation of Nature.

This was something of a shock, and served to strengthen the impression I had already acquired that the things of this world "are not always what they seem". It should be remembered that I had read no science at this time, though I was already twenty-one, and was totally ignorant of the atomic theory. Round the corner, if I pursued this course, the most painful collapse of my life was awaiting me. Utterly ignorant of the implications, I read on, entranced, in that little library between the quadrangle and the lavatories, with the blue baize tablecloths, and the high round-headed windows, which had once been a chapel and was now a store for books.

The second of my books was *Scottish Philosophy*, by A. Seth Pringle-Pattison. Somewhere about the middle this proved to contain a proposition of a very fundamental character. The author pointed out that if there is truth in the theory of cause and effect; if, that is, events are indeed the effects of causes, then experience seems to suggest, further, that causes are generally not *less* powerful than their effects, but *more* so. In other words, behind the noblest known expressions of human genius, character and personality, there is likely to be a cause, somewhere, even nobler; and some cause, even more beautiful, behind the most beautiful manifestations of Nature that we have ever seen.

As I read these words, I asked myself whether this could be an indication, if nothing more, of the truth of the existence of God. I could see that it did not *prove* that God existed, but I did think that it had made it my reasonable duty to inquire further into that hypothesis, which I had in my own life so long dismissed as on balance probably untenable.

What I did, perhaps unfairly short-circuited matters. I decided to test this question further by practical methods. Church services were alleged to be the normal means of getting into touch with God and I determined to make a trial and see what would happen.

This was remarkably naïve and I laugh heartily now when I think of it: but what *did* happen? The obvious thing to which I had laid myself open—I met God in five days and fell in love with him. It was simply a love affair. Everybody knows that love affairs can end in the Divorce Court. I hope mine will not, but I have certainly put it to severe tests at various times.

I made this discovery in Radcliffe Square outside

Brasenose College, in a little chapel on the north side of Saint Mary's, the University Church, the church which had been Cardinal Newman's. I went there because the girl I was in love with used that church and I thought that what satisfied her must surely be the best I was likely to find for my experiment.

This girl was Barbara, younger daughter of the first Viscount Buckmaster, herself wonderfully sweet, clever and beautiful, and the daughter of quite the most wonderful man I have ever met. A life of the first Lord Buckmaster has not, as far as I know, yet been written. I will only say here that I have never in all my experience met anyone else who combined such an extraordinary degree of power, brilliance and purity of intention. He displayed a fourth quality, equally precious, but unfortunately it was not perhaps equally deep in his character—the quality of gaiety. To me it was an amazement to find him lumped with Lord Simon in Mr. M. Thomson's recent *Life of Lord Lloyd-George* as a "distinguished loiterer".

I met him first in the unpromising surroundings of the Tottenham Court Road Underground railway station. It was by appointment. I had no notion what he looked like, but there was no possibility of doubting which was the man. He was standing against the wall on the left of the entrance, in the sort of clothes he liked to wear, which might well have been worn by a Scottish ghillie. A roman face, a pair of startling opaque blue eyes, interrogated my character and I walked over to him without hesitation. There could not possibly be anybody else like him in the whole world. I never saw the ugly canopy over the pavement outside that station later in the raids on London without a jerk of excitement. Barbara, who later became my wife, was the sort of person such a man might be expected to have for a daughter. Much taller than he was, with a lovely head of rather coarse, curly hair, similar eyes, a brilliant intellect and the loyalest character, she had forced her way, from the most improbable beginnings, into the Anglo-Catholic wing of the Church of England.

There followed five months of perfect happiness; a holiday reading in Devonshire, a visit with Barbara to the Communist Colony in Gloucestershire (which I shall describe in a later chapter); summer evening walks with Barbara in the hayfields at Wood Eaton; above all, the never-failing delight and astonishment at having God for a friend. And then fell the most severe blow of the whole of my life. I was walking one afternoon up the right-hand side of St. Giles Street when I glanced upwards to my left and saw a man wearing a top hat coming down the street in the front seat on the upper deck of a bus. At that period, the tops of buses were open. The hat was at a rakish angle and suddenly my world gave way. I was struck down with the most appalling melancholy. It was as though a trigger had been sprung in my mind. The life by which I was surrounded collapsed and became as unsubstantial as the backcloth of a scene in a theatre.

As I hope I have made plain, I had been struggling for

four years with a growing sense of the unreality of life as I knew it. That a man should actually be moving along in a top hat, and a short black coat, a sort of living symbol of unreality, surveying from the roof of a bus, the world he had created, was for me, at that stage, too much. The horror never left me for five years. It lasted intermittently, for fourteen years and in 1929 it nearly killed me.

CHAPTER SEVEN

THE MINE IN BARKING CREEK

"Super flumina Babylonis"
Ps. 136

Brentwood was all very well, and a useful experience, but it will have been noticed that I had not yet actually touched a live magnetic mine. From Brentwood, I went on to a series of disappointing cases. I was quite unable to undo any part of any one of the next three mines on my list. The spanners in the tool box bent double in my hands; the bolts remained unmoved, as though they were dummies. In desperation, I acquired a set of steel spanners from a garage. I even took a sledge hammer to one mine—a small one, weighing only half a ton, which had rolled right down a hill into a copse near Chelmsford. This was madness, but I was becoming much afraid that I should be dismissed and sent back to Brighton. For three nights I returned to the Admiralty to report failure. But it was all, in fact, a blessing in disguise: day after day other members of the party were bringing in every sort of exhibit—hydrostatic clocks, coils of copper spring, fuses, booby traps—and the pile on the table in the room upstairs grew steadily. The result was that when at last I was able to open a mine, I

56

LT.-COMDR. JOHN MILLER G.C. R.N.V.R.
1941

was able to recognize much of what I found and to avoid making certain serious mistakes.

In the beginning and later with any unfamiliar mine, our method was to station our sailor at least a hundred yards away behind some cover—a rise in the ground or a broken wall. He carried a notebook and a pencil. Then, taking a selection of tools, we started work, shouting to the sailor before each move and explaining as precisely as possible what we were going to do. We would call, for example, "I am now going to cut a blue lead." The sailor would write this down in his book and raise his hand when he had finished. If the mine exploded, he could return to the Admiralty, show his notes, and say, "Next gentleman must not cut a blue lead." Every possible operation was carried out from two hundred yards away on the end of a long line. The film of Nigel Balchin's book, *The Small Back Room*, gives a good impression of what it is like to tackle a bomb, but it is shocking to see the hero do several things six inches away from his face, which could quite easily have been done from what in that case would have been the safe distance of a hundred yards.

Our instructions were that no sailor was to be allowed on a mine; for various reasons, the work was to be done only by officers. The sailors, however, used to beg to be allowed to attempt a mine; and I am sorry to say that I know of more than one case where a sailor actually did a job, particularly when we were faced with an exceptionally heavy programme. There were other cases which no one man could have tackled alone, and then our sailors insisted on helping us. One such was the mine in Barking Creek.

The first problem was how to reach it. The bottom of the creek consisted of deep, soft, black mud. We put a foot upon the mud at the edge of the creek, and sank in immediately. Some hundreds of yards away on the left was a large timber yard, and from there we borrowed some long planks; the mud bore the weight of a plank, but the moment we stepped on the first one, it sank under the surface. Had we known then as much as we did later we would have tried a "Swiss Roll" or carpet of wire and kapok. As it was, we withdrew, baffled, to the timber yard with our planks. In conversation there we heard that one of the directors of the yard knew more about the Barking river than any other living man and we made up our minds to call on him. We discussed the possibility of closing a lock for the duration of the necessary operations, but in the course of our talk we gathered that the centre of the creek consisted of a hard chalk bed on which it was possible to walk. We decided to approach the mine up-stream, by water, and attempt to wade the last few hundred yards, up the middle of the channel.

We went round to the offices of the Borough Engineer, explained our plans, and asked whether Barking possessed a municipal park with a lake in it and if so, whether by any chance he could lend us a small canoe. He certainly could lend us a canoe, said the engineer; and pressing a bell he ordered one to be placed upon a lorry and held at our disposal for as long as we should need it.

We returned to the Admiralty and reported the facts to Captain Currey. The Captain pointed out that after being under water for so long the mine was almost certainly switched on and instructed us not to touch it until the situation had been further considered. After some discussion we persuaded him to let us try at any rate to reach the mine the next day, if only in order to try out the approach and make a report on the details, such as the probable nature of the mine, the position in which it was lying, what sections were exposed, and for how long they showed above the surface on either side of dead low water. Having secured the Captain's reluctant consent to this, we knew we had put ourselves in a strong position, for once on the spot we should be entitled to use our discretion.

The morning's assignment struck Tuckwell and me as exceedingly dangerous. As the Captain had said, the mine was almost certainly alive and there would in any case be no possibility of running away, if that proved to be necessary, We decided to drive to my home in Northamptonshire for the night; I wanted to see the place once again, and say goodbye. The old house stands in the long village street at King's Cliffe, in that lovely Cotswold stone country between Peterborough and Kettering. The name means "the King's Valley" and the place is so called because King John had a hunting-box here from which he would hunt in Rockingham Forest, and the ramps of his fish ponds still block the stream below the house. Built in Tudor times, mullioned windows on the street attest its date, but southwards towards the garden, running down from the house to the stream, wide eighteenth-century sashes lie open to the sun and give on to a fascinating prospect of dahlia beds, arches and tables and birds, of yew, mulberry trees and walnuts, and behind, across the stream, gently rising paddocks and the slopes leading to Fotheringay. At night, in peace-time, over to the west, above the high garden wall, the sky would be red with the glare of Corby steelworks; but the gases above the furnace were extinguished with the declaration of war and as Tuckwell and I, lugging our dark bags of tools, stole in through the stable gate on to the lawn at one o'clock in the morning, the facade of the house stood glimmering softly in nothing but pale moonlight. I was bending down to pick up pebbles to throw at the window when a clear voice from high up on the facade demanded our business. It was my cousin Clare, to whom this book is dedicated, who had heard our entry and conceived us to be burglars.

The Manor House received us into its tranquillity. To Tuckwell many of these things were new; but I myself was for a few hours reminded of the happiest of the past—of riding in Rockingham Forest or over the wide sheep-pastures lying open to the sky; of Mass in the great house at Laxton, in the chapel which had once been a vinery; of summer days deep in the dahlia beds, snipping the dying flowers from the stalks over our heads; of the folk-dancing at Rockingham Castle, the high lawn encircled with a stone parapet looking far out over the valley of the Welland; and then further afield but recalled by the pictures of King's Cliffe, three other Catholic country-house chapels in my memory—Tichborne, near Winchester, Wardour in Wiltshire and loveliest of all, Ugbrooke, near Exeter, the home of Clare's mother's family, the Cliffords. The first Lord Clifford of Chudleigh was Prime Minister to King Charles the Second, but at the hazard of his office and even his head became a Catholic. He possessed a truly remarkable tolerance of mind; some of his letters might have been written at the end of the nineteenth century instead of at the end of the seventeenth; and this detachment has remained in the family. They retained their Catholicism throughout the penal times. The chapel at Ugbrooke, like that at Tichborne, was concealed, for fear of attack from passing Protestant soldiery. Even to-day, it would never be noticed by a visitor who did not know it was there. Round the corner of the house, in a yard which clearly gives on to the kitchen quarter, a flight of a few worn steps leads up to an old glass-topped door. Behind the glass a torn lace curtain hangs upon a string. It is obviously a scullery. But push the door open and you will find yourself in a lofty little basilica, lined with marbles and faintly scented with incense.

As often in such places, the family are provided with seats in an upper gallery, with private access from the house. In this case, the access is from the library; the door opens through the shelves and is masked with false books. A glance at the titles will reveal such selections as:

THE SMALL NUMBER OF THE ELECT
by St. Just (—) in
THE MIRROR OF VIRTUE
by St. Boniface.

Titles perhaps not really to be enjoyed except by those who are accustomed to High Church jokes, and further have known what it is to scramble into Mass, only just before the Gospel, pyjamas mercifully hidden from the congregation below by the parapet of the gallery. (I should perhaps just explain that you have not technically "heard Mass" if you are not in time for the Gospel.)

Consoled by these memories of the Catholic faith, drawn so closely and so sweetly into the everyday life of the family, I left with the first light of the next day for Barking.

Arrived at Barking, we collected our canoe and drove down the creek to the point where it joins the main stream and boarded a station of the River Fire Service. The officer in command immediately agreed to help; and Tuckwell and I, our kit and canoe were put on a fire-float and on the last of the falling tide we motored off up the creek towards the position where the mine was lying.

It was an unpromising afternoon, in early winter, cold, windy and wet with frequent rainstorms. About half a mile below the mine, the firefloat grounded. The area still covered by water was rapidly narrowing. We said good-bye to the Captain and the crew and dropped over the side into our canoe. We were both wearing oilskins and long gumboots, reaching to the thighs. We turned the canoe's nose into the stream and started paddling up the muddy current. We paddled for about a hundred yards, and stuck. We swung our legs over the side and felt the bottom. We turned to each other and smiled slightly—there was a comparatively firm chalky track, about two yards across, in the middle of the creek, where the last of the current was flowing. We stood up, grabbing the canoe between us, and paused to take stock. It was an eerie position. The winter afternoon was drawing on. On either side, a great flat of black mud was ticking faintly as the water drained from it. On the right, the huge wharf of the timber yard blocked the sky. On the left, the wall of the creek seemed to lean over us. We felt very deep down, and likely to suffocate. The air was wet and stinking. A short way ahead, one of the London sewers was discharging a cascade of yellow foam.

We turned up-stream and ploughed slowly forward. Just above the sewer's mouth we began to slide into a pit: thoroughly alarmed, we thought it would not after all be possible to walk along the bottom, but it suddenly occurred to us that this must be the crater formed by a bomb. We climbed into the canoe, paddled some yards, and found our diagnosis was correct; our paddles struck bottom on the far side of the crater, and we resumed our former method of progress, dragging the canoe between us on the shallow current.

Rounding a slight bend, sweating inside our oilskins, we sighted the black rim of the mine. We exchanged a glance of triumph; the mine was right on the edge of the chalk fairway. We pushed cautiously forward till we stood abreast, and listened. The water was swirling and gurgling around the parachute housing. We hitched the canoe to the tail. The mine was still stuck in the mud by the nose but with the passage of two tides had fallen over sideways and was lying at an acute angle to the surface. To all appearances it was of a standard magnetic type. The main fuse was on top, the upper part just showing.

It was obvious that if all went well we should just have time before the tide rose to extract the fuse and then open up the main passages; and it seemed clear that had it been possible to consult the Admiralty it would have been agreed that in the circumstances this was the best course to pursue. I decided to do it.

At this point I regained, with an effort, an official manner and asked Tuckwell to withdraw. I said he had better take cover on the bank opposite the mine and make the usual notes. He said he thought it should hardly be necessary for him to point out that it would take him at least two hours to reach the place I had indicated. Besides, I should have to work under about a foot of water, and would need someone to hand me the tools. I should have to stand over the mine all the time—we could hardly drag our feet through the soft going at this point—and it

64

would be quite impossible in the time available to get away to do anything from a distance. In short, if my number was up, he would like to be with me. The tide was showing signs of slackening. There was no time to lose. I smiled and we got to work.

I unscrewed the ring which secured the fuse in position. In the ordinary way, once this was off I should have attached a line to the fuse and pulled it out from a safe distance. We exchanged a look, and I grabbed the fuse and whipped it out with a jerk which flung it away over my shoulder into the water. Nothing happened.

After a very brief pause we set about the rest of the work, putting our faith in the non-magnetic tools supplied by H.M.S. *Vernon*. By the time we had extracted what appeared to be the more important elements the tide had risen above my elbows and we were working below water. It was raining hard but the mud was covered. We got into our canoe and paddled straight across the wharf, and climbed to the top, rather shakily—the ladder was very high, and slimy with seaweed and mud.

Along the wharf was a range of enormous cranes. The wharf had been evacuated while we were working on the mine but several of the crane drivers had taken up a position from which they could watch. We explained that we had pulled out one fuse but there were other dangerous elements in the carcase; would anybody risk helping us to drag the mine from the creek and get it up on to the wharf for the final operation? Without hesitation the whole party volunteered: manning one of the

E   65

largest cranes, they paid out a length of cable. To the end of the cable we attached a stout rope and with this Tuckwell and I were lowered over the edge of the wharf in the canoe into the water. We pulled the rope over to the mine, made it fast round one end of the carcase, signalled the crane, and the huge cylinder was dragged slowly over the mud to the foot of the wharf. Tuckwell and I, the mine and the canoe all came out of the creek together on the end of the cable, and the final stages of the work were completed, in rain, but nevertheless in comparative comfort.

THE MINE AT BARKING CREEK

CHAPTER EIGHT

SAINT TERESA ON A BOOKSHELF
1926

"Si terrena dixi vobis et non creditis, quomodo si dixero caelestia?"
S. John 3

Those who are acquainted with the normal course of the spiritual life, as well as those who have a knowledge of psychiatry, will be able to form their own conclusions as to what happened to me in St. Giles Street. At the time, both these things were a good deal above my head. I was, however, dimly aware that I might have landed myself in what John Bunyan calls the "Slough of Despond". In my parents' house, there were as far as I knew few books about religion except for the Bible itself and a copy of Bunyan's *Pilgrim's Progress*. We had enjoyed nothing more as children than hearing my mother reading the *Pilgrim's Progress* as we went to bed. We knew that it was an allegory of life in this world, but somehow we never realized that the next life could begin for us before "the trumpets sounded on the other side". We assumed that the pilgrimage had to be undertaken in trust, from a sense of duty, perhaps merely from a fear of being overwhelmed with others in the City of Destruction. I did not know that this life could be turned into a pilgrimage by the fact that I should meet the ruler of Heaven here. For years I had joined in the glorious singing of the Psalter at Rugby School, and knew the New Testament well, both in Greek and English, but that one could "love" God, in the sense that one could love a girl, had never entered into my head. The *Pilgrim's Progress* is so highly allegorical that the neophyte can hardly use it as a first guide. I think parents might read to their children at some time some extracts from that very charming and straightforward account of the different Counter-Reformation schools of mysticism written by Dom Bede Frost of the Anglican Benedictine Order, under the title *The Art of Mental Prayer*. If you take a sheet of paper and set out in parallel columns the stages of an interview with God as outlined by Frost from each of the disciplines—Carmelite, Ignatian, Salesian, Oratorian, etc.—you will, I think, inevitably come to the conclusion that there is agreement on essentials; and further, from the book as a whole there emerges a clear "map" of the spiritual life as it has taken shape in the post-Reformation period.

It is difficult to understand why these important things are so completely unknown to the average educated Englishman: even to the average English Roman Catholic. The spiritual unreality with which so many so ineffectually struggle must be almost entirely due to the fact that people do not now make use of the maps which the experience of many generations has provided for them.

It should be understood that I had read literally no

mystical theology in 1925. I had first-hand experience of falling in love with God: but no notion whatever that this was a common experience, or that anything had been written about it. Terrible though the rest of my situation might be, at least the presence of God never left me and I simply lived in it.

About this time I was staying with my friend Tony Disney, now Director of Economics and Trade in the Sudan, at Burnham Overy Staithe on the north coast of Norfolk. Nobody could be saner than Disney and I hope no one will suppose that he is in any way responsible for any of this. We were there to read Locke, and to enjoy some sailing in the creeks, and some walking in the exquisite country which edges the sea along the whole of that coast-line. From a shelf in the Moorings Hotel I happened to pull out an English translation of the Auto-biography of Saint Teresa of Spain—not the "Little Flower" of Lisieux, but Saint Teresa of Avila. This was my first introduction to post-Reformation, or indeed to any traditional Catholic spirituality. I do hope that any non-Catholic who may try it after reading these pages will do so with great caution. I was myself astounded, and at first actually repelled, by what I read there. But the basic fact was that here was an open statement by somebody else, who was, after all, an historical character and a canonized saint, that she herself had fallen in love with God and what is more, had run into great spiritual pain as a result of it. This began to look better, though I had certainly got into a very peculiar *galère* indeed. I have always been intensely thankful that I had read some modern psychology before I ever saw Saint Teresa's *Life* or indeed any other orthodox books on mystical prayer. It gives one a certain basis of criticism which enables one to discount to a prudent degree some of the extreme element which seems invariably to invade these books. Without it, I think, any educated person who came to them for the first time as an adult would be forced to drop them, with a considerable feeling of revulsion. The subject needs radically to be re-written for the present day. That, presumably, is why it does not at present form part of current English thought.

Christian mystical writing, in long patches, is exceedingly dismal: nobody seems to have explained why. Post-Reformation Catholic mystical writing is (if possible) even more dismal than its pre-Reformation counterpart. It must certainly be important not to enjoy life on this earth so generously as to have no time to consider those painful elements which are as truly a part of it as the joy. Perhaps in the ages of Faith this was a real danger, and meditation upon our own sin, and upon Christ's Passion, may have been a good way to check it, and a good starting point, leading on to other things. But in these days sorrow, pity and doubt are so much a part of our lives that it seems strange that those who undertake the religious life do not choose to stress the happier side. This happier side must surely be one of the main reasons for setting out to get to know God. Saint Teresa, Saint John of the Cross, Saint Catherine of Genoa, all in their

BERNINI'S PORTRAIT OF S. TERESA
RECEIVING THE WOUND OF LOVE

(*Church of S. Maria della Vittoria, Rome*)

own ways present an appalling picture of the type of mental life which in the past has been associated with Christian mysticism. Yet when they throw aside every-thing but their experience of the love of God, their writings are entrancing.

Saint Teresa says in her *Life* (chapter 8) that no one has ever taken God for a friend without being rewarded; "mental prayer," she goes on, "in my view, is nothing but friendly intercourse, and frequent solitary converse, with Him who we know loves us . . . you will gladly endure the troubles which arise from being with so much One Who is so different from you. . . . Oh Joy of the angels, how I long to be wholly consumed in love for Thee." A great part of her *Life* is taken up with an account of the stages of prayer, which she divides in this case into four. "Having gone through so much myself," she says (chapter 13), "I am sorry for those who begin with books alone, for it is extraordinary what a difference there is between understanding a thing and knowing it by ex-perience." I will quote two examples which she gives of prayer in the first stage, and one extract from her account of the fourth, for though it would seem that this last at any rate is too intimate to be printed, printed it has been, by ecclesiastical order, and if by being printed again, in this new context, it will reach some who other-wise would never have seen it; well, then by that alone, my writing of these tales will be justified. I shall quote, by permission, from Professor E. Allison Peers' lovely and sensitive translation (*London:* Sheed & Ward, 1946.)

71

"Often," writes the Saint (chapter 14) "when I was a beginner (and may the Lord grant that I have in fact even now begun to serve His Majesty—but I mean a beginner by comparison with what I shall say about my life hereafter) it used to give me great delight to think of my soul as a garden and of the Lord as walking in it. I would beg Him to increase the fragrance of the little buds of virtue which seemed to be beginning to appear and to keep them alive so that they might bloom to His glory—for I wanted nothing for myself—and I would ask Him to prune away any of them He wished to, for I knew that the plants would be all the better if He did."

I quote the second example from this degree, though the first alone should really be enough, because though lovely in itself it shows some of that concentration upon sadness which I have warned my readers they must expect in these writings. "My method of prayer was this (chapter 9). As I could not reason with my mind, I would try to make pictures of Christ inwardly, and I used to think I felt better when I dwelt on those parts of His life when He was most often alone. It seemed to me that His being alone and afflicted, like a person in need, made it possible for me to approach Him. I was particularly attached to the Prayer in the Garden, where I would often go to keep Him company. I would think of the sweat and the affliction He endured there. I wished I could have wiped that grievous sweat from His face but I remember I never dared to resolve to do so, for the gravity of my sins stood in the way. I used to remain with Him there as long as my thoughts permitted it."

Of the fourth degree she says (in part, chapter 20), "In these raptures the soul seems no longer to animate the body, and thus the natural heat of the body is felt to be very sensibly diminished: it gradually becomes colder, though conscious of the greatest sweetness and delight. No means of resistance is possible ... my soul has been borne away, and indeed as a rule my head also, without my being able to prevent it: sometimes my whole body has been affected, to the point of being raised up from the ground. This has happened only rarely; but once, when we were together in choir, and I was on my knees and about to communicate, it caused me the greatest distress. It seemed to me the most extraordinary thing and I thought there would be a great deal of talk about it; so I ordered the nuns (for it happened after I was appointed Prioress) not to speak of it. On other occasions, when I have felt the Lord was going to enrapture me (once it happened during a sermon, on our patronal festival, when some great ladies were present), I have lain on the ground and the sisters have come and held me down, but none the less the rapture has been observed. I besought the Lord earnestly not to grant me any more favours which had visible and exterior signs; for I was exhausted by having to endure such worries and after all (I said) His Majesty could grant me that favour without its becoming known ... very often a desire unexpectedly arises, in a way which I cannot explain. And this desire, which in a single moment penetrates to the very depths of the soul, begins to weary it so much that the soul soars upwards, far above itself and above all created things, and God causes it to be so completely bereft of everything that, however hard it may strive to do so, it can find nothing on earth to keep it company. Nor does it desire company. It would rather die in its solitude. Others may speak to it, and it may itself make every possible effort to speak, but all to no avail; do what it may, its spirit cannot escape from that solitude. God seems very far from the soul then, yet sometimes He reveals His greatness in the strangest way imaginable; this cannot be described—nor, I think, believed or understood—save by those who have experienced it. For it is a communication intended, not to comfort the soul but to show it the reason why it is wearied—namely, that it is so far away from the Good which contains all that is good within itself.

"In this communication the desire grows, and with it the extremity of loneliness experienced by the soul with a distress so subtle and yet so piercing that, set as it is in that desert, it can, I think, say literally, as the Royal Prophet said, when he was in the same state of loneliness (except that being a saint he may have been granted that experience by the Lord in a higher degree): "vigilavi, et factus sum sicut passer solitarius in tecto." "I have watched, and have become as a sparrow, all alone on a house-top." That verse comes to my mind at these

74

times in such a way that I feel it is fulfilled in myself; and it is a comfort to me to know that others, especially such a prophet as this, have experienced that great extremity of loneliness.

" . . . at other times I used to remember some words of Saint Paul, about his being crucified to the world. I do not say that this is true of me—indeed I know it is not—but I think it is true of the soul when no comfort comes to it from Heaven, and it is not in Heaven, and when it desires no earthly comfort, and it is not on earth either, but is, as it were, crucified between Heaven and earth; and it suffers greatly, for no help comes to it either from the one hand or from the other. For the help which comes to it from Heaven is, as I have said, a knowledge of God so wonderful, and so far above all that we can desire, that it brings with it greater torment. . . . It seems as though it were on the threshold of death, save that this suffering brings with it such great happiness that I know of nothing with which it can be compared . . . the soul realizes clearly that it wants nothing save its God; but its love is not centred upon any particular attribute of Him: its desire is for the whole of God and it has no knowledge of what it desires. By 'no knowledge' I mean that no picture is formed in the imagination; and, in my opinion, for a great part of the time during which it is in that state, the faculties are inactive: they are suspended by their distress, just as in union and rapture they are suspended by joy."

It is difficult to turn back from Saint Teresa's pages

to the ordinary world: but what I write has been written in the main in the hope that others will attempt to-day the same journey and I must, I suppose, leave 1560 for 1926 and its different circumstances.

It is possible that "souls" are predominantly "masculine" or "feminine" in their relations with the Almighty and this irrespective of their physical sex. Perhaps it is best for a "masculine" soul to start with a "masculine" type of writer—e.g. Saint John of the Cross—and for the others to begin with a "feminine" writer, which I should say Saint Teresa certainly is. By masculine, I mean those who naturally take the initiative with God, at any rate in the early stages. The others will probably find that God makes all the running. Perhaps the most attractive recent guide is Baron F. von Hugel. But even on the lowest flights of the ladder he offers—I would put *Letters to a Niece* as low as anything I know—there is much trouble and strain left about the steps. It may be necessary for the individual who undertakes this adventure to pass through both the dark nights, the night of the senses and the night of the soul, but if the nature of these experiences could be set out in up-to-date language and if the necessity for them could be shown in present-day terms, people might be spared unnecessary pain and hesitation, and might embark on these things more in the spirit in which they approach their dentists—knowing that it may well hurt, but that there will be no more pain than is necessary.

The Roman Missal, a unique framework for the religion

of daily life, is itself, on balance, a rather gloomy structure. I have a collection in the end-pages of mine of the lighter passages. One is from the epistle for September 8th, the Nativity of the Blessed Virgin (Proverbs viii)— "Dominus possedit me in initio viarum suarum . . . (in the Creation) . . . cum eo eram cuncta componens, et delectabar per singulos dies, ludens coram eo omni tempore, ludens in orbe terrarum et deliciae meae esso cum filiis hominum."

This mystical experience of God goes down the centuries like an African river, sometimes above the surface, sometimes below. The orthodox hesitate to approve the findings of Dr. Buchman's movement, but there can be no doubt that the members of the group have discovered it. The amount of direct conversation which can be had with God is quite astonishing. One learns to distinguish between one's own thoughts and those which are His.

It is surely important that the clergy should frankly state that this experience is something which is separable from the profession of Christianity. This would not be denied, but the tendency is to suggest that the Christian framework is so much the best that it is in effect the only possible one for a European. This may be so, but so many imagine that religion is not for them, simply because they do not care to commit themselves to a belief in the literal truth of the Incarnation. The theory that Christianity is the prerequisite of religion is still carried to such extremes in English life that it is impossible to proceed to the higher degrees of Freemasonry without first professing belief in it.

Be these things as they may, to revert to the story, from now on it was clear to me that it was the obvious duty of us all to treat every other human being as one of God's lovers, either actual or potential. For such, nothing but the best that the world has to offer could be good enough: and that best must, as far as possible, be impartially bestowed. The story continues for a while longer in a religious rather than in a political framework. I had yet to face the question whether it was not my duty to become a Roman Catholic. I also had to wait and see whether I could get out on the other side of the Slough of Despond, into a more normal state of mind.

CHAPTER NINE

THE GRAY'S INN ROAD

"Non est nobis colluctatio adversus carnem et sanguinem"
Ephes. 6

With October, November and December, 1940, the raids on London grew heavier and worse. When a parachute mine was reported down, even in the middle of London, every remaining house was cleared for a distance of four hundred yards all round until we gave the signal to return. People in Cardiff and Coventry, who were comparatively seldom raided, were inclined to ignore instructions; they used to trickle back to their houses for the most extraordinary reasons; they said they wanted to fetch a pipe or a parrot; and they interfered with our operations. In London we could rely on better discipline, but I only once found it so perfect that no one could be discovered who would enter the ring and show me where I should come upon the mine. This was in the Gray's Inn Road.

Tuckwell and I had driven up from the Staple Inn end. When we came to the ropes across the road we knew that we were not more than four hundred yards from our objective: we came to a halt and looked round for a policeman to let us through. Our kit was heavy and our practice was to drive as near as was reasonably consistent with safety so as not to have to carry it further than was necessary. At certain stages it was useful to have a car handy with the engine running. I never cared to put complete trust in Bickford's fuse.

Nobody was to be seen. The place was absolutely deserted. Ruined houses on either side, the usual glass in the street. I got out to shift the rope. It was about nine o'clock in the morning. Not a sound was to be heard. In the silence, the air raid sirens suddenly spoke.

This was a bit thick. There is something consoling in having one's mine pointed out by a policeman. It makes it seem rather more like a part of ordinary life. However, there was nothing for it and we should have to look for it ourselves. The address was "Kelvinator's".

We drove slowly up past the Royal Free Hospital and found "Kelvinator's" on the right. There was a show-room in front with a boarded-up plate glass window, the boards a good deal broken; and behind, a set of rambling factory premises.

Leaving the car in the road we climbed in through the window into the show-room. On the right, at the back, a passage led off behind; but so much debris, timber and so on, was blocking the way that we could not at once get through. We made our way out to the left. A reconnaissance through the factory buildings revealed nothing. There was no sign of a parachute in the roofs. The mine could not have exploded because the buildings were not sufficiently damaged. They were simply rather knocked about. Bricks and tiles and glass were lying about and the place felt eerie and dangerous.

As we were making our way out, puzzled and uneasy, we noticed a second passage running behind the showroom. This passage was absolutely dark. We looked at each other, and turned into it. We felt our way with our feet, moving very slowly, holding our arms out in front of us. The passage took a right-angle turn. We rounded the corner, and at one and the same moment we stopped. We had smelled a peculiar smell—the acrid smell given off by the explosive filling of a mine. I struck a match, and there in front of us was an extraordinary spectacle— the mine standing bolt upright, was completely blocking the passage. We stood stock still. The match burned down between my fingers. The blood was throbbing in my ears. I struck another, and saw that we hadn't a chance: the mine had come down slap into a dustbin which was standing in the passage: we could not get at the fuses.

The match dropped, we turned tail, ran back out of the passage into the daylight, put a couple of buildings between us and the mine and pressed ourselves, panting, under the lee of a wall.

Because of the special design of the mines which were then in use, the slightest vibration might be enough to explode them. True, I had myself taken a sledge hammer to one; but that had happened to be damaged in a particular manner and the normal reaction had not been set up. The problem in this case appeared to be insoluble.

The only conceivable way to deal with it was to fit tackle and hoist the mine up out of the bin: but even supposing one could successfully carry off the work of fitting the tackle, the first lift must be expected to detonate the mine. Supposing, again, that the thing could be lifted up, the nose was clearly jammed tight into the bin and the operation of knocking off the bin would surely detonate it. Though the mine could be hoisted from a distance once the tackle was fitted, how could we knock off the bin from a distance? And if the mine went up, as it surely must do, the buildings of the Royal Free Hospital would be severely damaged. The mine was practically touching the north wall.

I went back into the passage and had another look. To my delight, a second inspection showed that the mine was not in a dustbin at all. It was actually wrapped in some lead roofing sheet, for all the world like a bath-towel round a man's middle. It must have come down spinning on the end of its parachute and have picked up this sheeting as it crashed through the roof of the passage. Tha parachute had come down over the hole and was keeping out the light.

The only thing to do was carefully to unwrap the lead with my hands, hoping against hope that I could do so without setting up a detonation. It was particularly difficult, because I could only get to one side of the mine at once. It was necessary to pull away the lead a little on one side first, and then go round through the show-room to the other end of the passage and work on the other side. I could have asked Tuckwell to work on the other side, but it did not seem reasonable. He insisted, however, on helping to clear the debris from the show-room so that I could get at that end of the passage. This meant pulling away heavy timber and causing a lot of vibration, in a position from which we could not possibly have escaped.

The passage once cleared, I shut my mind off as best I could and worked away at the lead, first one side and then the other.

I got it loose on the floor, ran out and took a rest. We then made fast a rope to the lead and with the help of a party of firemen we dragged the stuff out from the passage from a safe distance. The only thing was that I had to go back to extract the fuses. It was a case of the same Box and Cox procedure, and I suppose this last phase could not have taken less than three-quarters of an hour. I do not recall any other mine in my experience which imposed so great a strain upon the will.

CHAPTER TEN

THE PLAIN CALLED EASE

"Ludens in orbe terrarum"
Prov. 8

Bunyan reveals that the way of the Christian was not always hard: true, By-Path Meadow was a seduction and nothing but the outlying domain of the Castle of Giant Despair, but the way itself ran along the River of God, across the Plain called Ease and over the Delectable Mountains and surely no Oxford undergraduate can miss any one of these.

The Communist Colony at Whiteway, near Stroud, was an object of universal horror to the respectable of the county. Barbara and I were a little shocked ourselves: but we decided that as impartial philosophers we ought at least to see it.

We had little difficulty in finding directions to the place. It occupied something like a hundred acres on the bare edge of the Cotswolds above the Severn Valley. About a dozen small houses of a poor type were dotted irregularly about. Broken down wire fencing, a poultry run or two and a general air of neglect created an unfavourable impression on our aristocratic souls. Summoning our courage, however, we knocked upon the first door. We received a warm if somewhat distracted welcome. Our hostess was just off to Stroud to sell her eggs, and could not find the Colony's wedding ring. People lived, at Whiteway at that time, in a state of "free union"—which of course Barbara and I, as philosophers, approved—but in order to spare the neighbour's feelings as much as possible the Colony had invested in one wedding ring, which was put on for visits to the outer world.

We were taken to see other members of the party. The first was studying a set of painted wooden cubes, about an inch each way. He was good enough to explain his object. Life, he said, was an affair of relations; if he could train himself to visualize all the possible relations between these twenty-odd cubes, all the possible permutations of position between them, he should be able to understand the world as a whole in a much profounder sense.

Our next acquaintance was of a different stamp. A young Frenchman, with a small dark beard, and by choice an artist, he had a large mercator projection of the world upon his wall. How the conversation got round to this map I cannot remember, but he proceeded to give us an absolutely first-class lesson on the geography of primitive man, in the style of H. G. Wells' history of the world. Anything of this kind was entirely new to me and I listened spellbound.

Later in life I came to have much to do with the settlement upon the land of people without resources. This first experience was something of a shock but it proved later not untypical of what has to be dealt with. We retired to Oxford in a sober but somewhat exultant frame of mind.

The Greek play at Bradfield must be better known than the Colony at Whiteway, and all I need perhaps recall of it now is the remarkable entrance upon the scene which was made by the Headmaster. The audience was seated upon woolsacks on the wide, shallow steps of a horseshoe amphitheatre. The stage consisted of the foreground of an ordinary Greek temple, empty and yellow in the sun. A dappled light fell through overhanging trees on to the men and women of the audience. Brilliant blue and red fans had been distributed with the programmes. Suddenly two figures walked on, one from each side; they were dressed as messengers, their slender limbs delicately painted with sunburn under lionskin capes. Each carried a long trumpet. A complete silence fell. Slowly the trumpeters raised their horns to the corners of the amphitheatre, blew a strident note, and called aloud "Euphemite, o politai"—"keep silence, o ye citizens". We expected the appearance of a god.

In the tense excitement which followed, we observed an extraordinary apparition. Dressed in a rusty black frock coat and an old top hat, in walked the Headmaster and seated himself upon a chair in the front part of the auditorium.

Oxford in my day was much affected by the ex-Service element. They did not mix well with the ex-schoolboys. Although I might naturally have gravitated into their company, I actually found myself among the "aesthetics". This was not because I had any powers of conversation, but simply because I dressed nicely. Peter Rufa once expressed a regard for one of my ties, a small pale jade silk. I remember my father-in-law's terror that he might have to take me to the House of Lords in a pair of blue whipcord plus-fours. He need not have been in the slightest degree alarmed, but it was typical of his courtesy that he would hesitate to order an undergraduate to change his trousers. He used to maintain that "everyone should be allowed to go to hell in their own way".

There was a certain amusement to be had even out of reading philosophy—or at least, out of attempting to write it. Every week the undergraduate in the philosophy school had the privilege of going alone, or possibly with another man at much the same stage, to the rooms of his tutor for an hour's discussion. This began with the reading of an essay written to order on a set subject. My own philosophy tutor was N. R. Murphy (later Principal of the college); he would sit smoking, with a large box of exceedingly expensive cigarettes beside him and it was found to be possible, by uttering some statement which was more than usually outrageous, or boring, to make him throw his cigarette suddenly into the fireplace and take another. Tutorials were assessed in terms of the number of cigarettes thus ejected. His criticism of my essays was that I seemed to live in a night in which all cows were black. Whether true or not in his sense, it was, alas, only too true in another.

An interesting fact about my Oxford was that it was indecent and ill-bred to belong to the Labour Club. But licensed and much-loved idiots like John Sutro might join the Communist Society—the October Club—and be sure of help from anyone handy in the event of a raid by the university proctors.

Myself, I always tried to retain some hold upon reality amidst all these goings on, and after two or three seasons on the river I was chosen to cox my college eight. To row down the river to the start, in blazer and cap, with a bouquet of red roses in one's lap, is an experience never to be forgotten. It was on the college barge in Eights week, 1925, that I was first introduced to my beloved Barbara. The introduction was effected by Oliver Fielding Clarke, who afterwards went and lived in an ashram in India. Coxing really meant a great deal of hard work in all sorts of weather. The cold of coxing a Torpid in the river below Sandford Lock in the middle of winter has to be felt to be understood. Incidentally we were the theme of a river rhyme which ran:

> There was once a Togger of Blank
> Whose cox ran her nose in the bank.

I don't think I had better print any more of it. The actual steering of a racing eight is like steering a large car on an icy road. One does it by cautiously skidding the tail. *Note*. "Torpid" or "Togger"—a racing eight-oared boat with fixed, not sliding seats; that is, a boat for those who are not yet expert in the art.

Much of the Oxford vacations were spent, by invitation, with Lord Buckmaster. Of him, since I knew and loved him so well, I must write a few more sentences here, though so poorly qualified to do justice to his record. If it is not betraying a confidence, I would like to record one interesting fact about him. He was Lord Chancellor in Mr. Asquith's Government in 1916, and it was understood in the family that in later years he was invited to join a Labour Government in the same capacity. He refused, and the reason he gave was that he had seen too much of Government Departments in the first war to be able to believe that Socialism, that is, direction of industry by civil servants, could ever possibly work. Barbara and I disapproved of this view very strongly, but it was absolutely impossible to shake him. Another dictum of his influenced me greatly and was to the effect that we had reached a stage at which the present large populations could not physically be supported except on the basis of mass production; whether we liked it or not, if we were going to allow these populations to continue to exist, mass production had come to stay. This in answer to "art and crafters", supporters of cottage industry and the small man. I was glad to bear this in mind later when I was involved in so many committee meetings over schemes for assisting the unemployed. Though law and religion, not economics, was the centre of his thought, he struggled gamely for years to make people believe that to extract reparations from Germany on the scale proposed after 1918 was perfectly impracticable.

Before the 1914-18 war, he had been making a very large income at the Chancery Bar, and his usual practice was to take a large house in Wales or in Scotland for a part of each year. In the years when I knew him, he was living in the main upon his Lord Chancellor's pension of £5,000 a year and so intensely scrupulous was he in all money matters that when he decided for a time to accept the chairmanship of a British South-American Petroleum Company, he insisted upon returning his pension to the public funds, though there was no obligation of any kind upon him to do so. He was renting at that time a small fishing box on the River Spey in Scotland, between Grantown and Aberlour and though to his distress neither Barbara nor I ever took to salmon fishing, superb as the opportunities were, we were often there at his invitation and would certainly have been very happy had we been able to bear being separated for any length of time from the more eclectic forms of worship of the Church of England. It was in Scotland, with selected legal or political cronies in the house, that he showed his sunniest side: even there, his mind retained its strongly biblical lilt, and he would tease us for being unable, for all our apparent piety, to identify any one of a myriad of obscure Old Testament characters at a moment's notice. He was utterly devoid of any feeling for distinctions of birth. On one occasion he made time to journey down and show us the four-roomed cottage immediately below Clapham Junction Station in which he lived as a boy, where he and his brother had to sleep in the space between the ceiling and the slates.

The Buckmasters were in fact an old armorial family but a biography seems to suggest that Lord Buckmaster's father—John Charles Buckmaster—was the illegitimate son of a man who sank in the end to the level of a drunken agricultural labourer. Lord Buckmaster spent large amounts of time, his unforgettable eloquence, his strength and his money to help forward schemes for improving the housing of the poor in North Kensington. He was indeed the most perfect example of true Liberalism, too brilliant and strong to believe all men to be equal but determined that so far as he could secure it, all should have reasonable conditions of life and those whose qualities deserved it, whether boys or girls, an opportunity to receive the best education. This is the man who has been accused of cynical opportunism in Parliament and, ignored, for reasons unknown, in nearly every big political biography of the time. It is tempting to take revenge by revealing his comments on some of the lesser of those other figures in great places whom we knew; but I have no permission to do so. Nor do I think it necessary to touch upon those tragedies which haunted his private life, which were unknown to the majority of the outer world, but would have crushed a man of less immeasurable strength of will and character and which a generation later have darkened my own life to say nothing of that of others, in ways which I do not wish to describe.

Just one more thing I may perhaps be permitted to

record as showing the extraordinary acuteness of his vision. In the last year of his life, in 1934, as he lay ill with the illness which killed him, he said to me, "John, you will live to see the grass growing in the streets of the City of London." This was the sort of remark which one hears with a feeling of some embarrassment, when it falls from the lips of a representative of an earlier generation. Candidly, one says to oneself, this is all very well, but of course people must occasionally wander a little.

In 1941, seven years later, there, in very truth, along the sides of what had been Milk Street, the grass was growing.

Barbara and I were married in December of 1926, but I could not get the mud of the Slough of Despond off me. I applied for a post in the Colonial Service, took the Tropical African Services course in Oxford and London and left for Nigeria in the middle of 1927.

CHAPTER ELEVEN

LONDON BRIDGE

"Electi mei non laborabunt frustra"
Isai. 65

Tuckwell and I were both awarded the George Cross for our adventure at Barking. By 1941, many of our original squad were wearing the blue ribbon with a silver cross. I was seldom in the company of less than two other holders of the distinction and on many occasions there were four or more of us in one taxi. It was a little embarrassing, because in effect the awards were made on our personal account of what had happened; we worked alone and we alone could report the circumstances. The squad themselves were inclined to consider that really either all should have the cross or none; the same degree of courage was required to perform certain operations, whether the mine was "easy" or "difficult". In practice, we classified a mine as "difficult" if there was no prospect of escape if things began to go wrong and the clock fuse started.

In one of the Admiralty files there is a fascinating discussion of courage and its degrees. Many of the minutes are in the handwriting of famous men. We were shown this file, in order that we might learn the principles upon which officers and men of the Royal

Navy were recommended for decorations. We decided that an officer ought to be recommended for the highest decoration if the mine was difficult in two senses; first because there was no means of escape and second because the condition or nature of the mine was peculiarly dangerous, that is, for example, if it was damaged or of a new design. If a mine were merely one or the other, an officer might be recommended for a decoration of a lower class, and if it was just a mine, with no special feature, then it must be regarded as a part of the ordinary day's work, like signing a letter in the R.N.O.'s office in Lerwick in the Shetlands. Almost inevitably, in course of time, every officer who stayed in the section came to be recommended for the Cross. Lord Chatfield, the Chairman of the inter-Services committee through which all recommendations passed, was heard one day to remark that the George Cross could not be treated as a Long Service Medal for members of the Land Incident Section, as our party was officially named. There was also a ruling that there could be no such thing as a "bar" to the Cross, a ruling which those of us who were recommended for a bar thought very reasonable. The fact was that we knew we were all on a level and we were troubled that some of us received decorations while others did not.

In many cases, it was necessary, whatever the risk to the officer, to prevent a mine from detonating, if possible. These were cases in which damage "could not be accepted". One such was the mine on the viaduct outside London Bridge Station.

I set off for London Bridge early on the usual cold and rainy morning. All trains were stopped and the station was deserted except for a small party of officials in the ticket office. The mine was stated to be lying against the wall of a signal box which controlled the electrical signalling system for a considerable distance down the line.

I walked down over the end of the platform and picked my way between the rails towards the box. I disliked these assignments on electric railways: in the agitation of the moment, I could never keep my mind on avoiding the live lines, which was probably unnecessary but I used to think it advisable on principle. There are certain physical reactions to fear. Most people have reached the stage when it is necessary to piss, but it is possible that not all have proved for themselves that fear can knock a further stage out of them. Privacy, on a mine, was never a trouble, but it was inconvenient when you had so little warning that there was no time to take down your trousers.

A first glance at this mine showed that I was in for difficulties. It was on its nose, almost upright, in a re-entrant angle in the wall of the signal box. The parachute was not in the way—it was caught high up around some projecting metalwork—but the opening of the passage containing the clockwork fuse was on the under side and facing in towards the wall. It was impossible to risk moving the mine, and there was only just room to push my head between the side of it and the brickwork of the signal box. The only way to set about it was to lie on my back, gently wriggle in my head and arms and work with my mouth and eyes at a distance of about six inches from the opening. The rain had made a pool where I had to lie and I could not afford the time or the risk of digging a drain to take the water away. I was certainly attracted to mines, but had not so far felt impelled actually to kiss one. The psychological reaction to lying beneath a mine, at close quarters, was distinctly unpleasant. It was obvious that if the clock started to run I could not hope to escape; and there was something distasteful in being blown up, downwards.

It was my normal practice, standing by a mine, to sign myself with the sign of the Cross. If the mine was really very bad indeed, I didn't do it; fiddling of any kind seemed unnecessary. I did not sign myself in Kelvinator's passage, but I did here. Had I known what was going to happen, I might not have done.

I wriggled in under the mine and got a spanner in between my face and the big screw-threaded ring nut which held the fuse into its position. I had hardly moved the nut a quarter of a turn when I heard the little fizzing sound which showed that the clock inside had started. I knew that it would be quite impossible to unscrew the nut from that position before the twenty-two seconds were up, even supposing I had that allowance of time. The only thing to do was to start wriggling clear and try to get away up the line before the detonation. Much to my surprise, I got out and was well up the platform before anything happened.

Nothing did happen.

I pulled myself together and walked back to have a look. Obviously the clock was damaged and must have stuck after the first round or so. The situation did, after all, offer an element of hope; the clock might be so firmly stuck that with care it might be extracted. I wriggled in again and gave the ring another turn. The same noise. I managed to get away and ran up the line again. Nothing happened.

Rather dizzy with fright I walked into the ticket office and explained what was going on. The station master poured me out a cup of tea. I decided that there could not be any reasonable chance of escape a third time and in the circumstances the sensible thing to do was to get under the mine once more, if I could, and stay there, turning the nut as fast as possible. The mine must now be so dangerous that even if left to itself it must almost certainly detonate. In other words, "damage" *had* now to be "accepted" and my plan offered the only conceivable prospect of success.

The fizzing started again the moment I had my spanner on the ring. Two more turns and the ring was off. It suddenly struck me that the fizzing had stopped. So far, so good, after all; and I reflected that there was really no reason now why I should not be a little more careful. The clock must have jammed again in the last turn and I might now see whether the thing could not be pulled out from a distance in the regulation manner. I had my line in my teeth. I took the final risk of plugging the end

G 97

of it into the fuse, wriggled clear and dashed away towards the platform.

At the end of the line, I gave it a tweak; luck held and the fuse dropped out with a tinkle. The little yellow primer fell clear and rolled an inch or two away from the detonator.

My sailor and I looked at the pieces. I must spoil the story by giving some hint of what had happened. The clock had not moved a single turn. At that stage in our operations we were using air pressure to immobilize a part of the mechanism of those mines. The pitch filling in one section of this particular fuse had not been put in properly. The fizzing I had heard was my own air, escaping under pressure past the ring, when the ring was shifted. There had been a film of moisture in the passage.

We put our pieces in the car and drove back to the Admiralty to examine them at leisure. That fizzing had betrayed a dangerous weakness in our methods, and from that time onwards we abandoned air pressure altogether and used more direct methods.

CHAPTER TWELVE

NIGERIA
1927-28

"In omnibus requiem quaesivi. Tunc dixit mihi Creator omnium 'in Jacob inhabita, in Israel hereditare et in electis meis mitte radices'."
Eccli. 24

The Secretariat, in Lagos, Nigeria, in which I found myself, gave me a pre-view of the full scope of a British colonial government. I was made to read the annual report of every department of State and condense them into one single annual report for the whole Government. Americans do not always seem to understand that the British Empire does not exist, and that there is really no such thing as a British colonial government. What I mean is that the British do not "rule", nor do their colonial governments "govern". British administration is negative rather than positive; it is a matter of little more than keeping a ring. A feature of this is that the British usually try to keep the ring as much in the interests of the native population as of their own nationals. This perhaps explains why British administration is not more unpopular than it is, and also how it is that the colonial governments have always been able to find a supply of recruits of a good type for the Colonial

Service. The weakness of it has been that both types of "subject" have been expected to make their own running within the framework provided. The administration has never been personally interested in economics. If its members have known anything at all about "business", they have thought in terms of trade rather than industry; and the revenue of every colony has been largely exacted from that eccentric source, *duties on imports*. The result has been that no British colonial dependency has ever been properly developed.

I travelled out to Africa with an Oxford friend from my own college who had also joined the Nigerian Service. Shortly after we arrived in Lagos, I saw him off on his journey to a provincial station. In complete darkness he climbed down some steps on the river bank and crawled into a native dug-out canoe. A paraffin hurricane lamp burned under a tarpaulin hood amidships. His boxes were put aboard, and utterly alone, except for six African natives who formed the crew, he left for his station in the mangrove swamps behind the coast-line. At Oxford, he had lived in one of the yellow brick houses of Wellington Square. The fact that a Government official could travel in this fashion seemed to me to prove that the British administration in Nigeria was not un-popular in 1927.

After six months or so in the Secretariat I chose the Education Department as my niche. This was a little bizarre, as members of the Education Department were not regarded as gentlemen in any full sense of the word in 1927, if indeed they are now; but Barbara and I did not care much about that. We wanted to do something constructive.

Unfortunately, it was not correct to have anything to do, socially, with Africans. We summoned up our courage to brave this ban (it was only a convention, not a Government order) and we made friends with a girl called Oyinkan Abayomi. She was the daughter of a well-to-do African merchant in Lagos, Sir Kitoyi Ajasa. Her husband had been an African barrister and was said to have been shot in open court, in somewhat sensational circumstances. Oyinkan herself had been brought up in a convent in France: she was exquisitely beautiful, slender and olive-skinned and dressed charmingly in Paris frocks. We got to know her through her little daughter Tudi who used to call on us to eat chocolate biscuits. To visit Sir Kitoyi in an evening was an experience. He lived in a stone villa overlooking the racecourse. Under a large bread-fruit tree on the lawn behind the house there was always a big brass tray of drinks on a cane-legged table. Round the tray was a ring of basket chairs. The older ladies of the house, tightly wrapped from head to foot in coloured silks and cottons, were laid in the chairs like so many coloured golf umbrellas. They neither moved nor spoke. Sir Kitoyi, dressed in an ordinary dinner-jacket suit and a grey and white check cloth cap, welcomed his guests with a warm gesture. "Help yourself," he would cry, "this is Libairty Hall." All sorts of people would drop in and talk, all Africans, of course, all prominent in business and all profoundly interesting to Barbara and me. It never seemed to us that these prominent Africans were any different mentally, from Englishmen, but we were admittedly in contact with the men who were at the top of the tree. The wealth of these men was great and their connections were correspondingly wide and varied, by no means confined to Africa.

Among the Englishmen in Lagos, quite the most notable was Upton Fitz Herbert Ruxton, Lieutenant-Governor of the Southern Provinces. His minutes on Secretariat papers filled me with delight, and the authorities, oddly enough, with fury. He had a detached, upper-class English mind, he was the son of an Admiral, he had been long alone in the bush and he combined in one person the man of affairs and the saint. Some prominent characters there are in the Catholic Church who receive the title "Venerable", but lacking wit, are never promoted to full saintly honours. Ruxton had an exquisite sense of humour and a mind like a rapier. He married a French-woman, a Paris royalist, who visited Charles Maurras in prison. She lived with her husband in Nigeria, on condition that their holidays should be spent in civilization, in France.

The affairs of the Anglican Church in Nigeria were in the hands of a Protestant mission. The Bishop wore a blazer and the church services were devoid of any traces of Ritualism. Ruxton, like ourselves, attended such Communion services as were conducted, and to our expert eye he was obviously an Anglo-Catholic. He never made his Communion from one end of a tour of of duty to the other. The reason—eccentric to some— was that the parson did not believe in hearing confessions. We understood this perfectly. As we mercifully both spoke French, we were given the great privilege of joining the family. This included a large number of Siamese cats, to which I have been devoted ever since. Mrs. Ruxton had brought out from Paris a deep and costly feather bed. She found it too hot and it was given to the cats.

As daily Mass was not to be had—except, of course, at the French cathedral—I made a practice in Nigeria of reading the Anglican Communion service each morning, with the insets proper to the day. The French cathedral was a huge barn-like structure of brick with a broken cement floor and open spaces for windows. In the presbytery there was an interesting account of the early days of the Mission and of the great hardships, and casualties, of the first priests and nuns. The first converts carried the bricks for the cathedral across the swamps in baskets on their heads for miles. I used to slip in there on my way back from the office at night to pay a visit to the Blessed Sacrament. One of the African clerks who was walking with me one night asked me if I was a member of that church. I said no, but I used it. "Too much idol," he answered and strode away.

We calculated that there was one separate Protestant church organization in Southern Nigeria at that time for every day of the year, including the American missions and the various indigenous African churches, polygamous and others. I once called in the company of a District Officer, at a church run by an African pastor about fifteen miles back into the forest behind Lagos. The vast graceful cotton trees hung far overhead. The pastor showed us round, and as we passed the altar—I should say, in this case, the Holy Table—my companion raised his nose slightly and sniffed. He tried the handle of a door in the wall. The pastor told us it was nothing but a vestry. My friend insisted on having the door opened. We walked in, and there, on a stone immediately behind the wall at the back of the altar, was the fresh blood of a cock. The pastor was doubling the parts.

I caught chronic malaria in Lagos and was invalided home in 1929. First-hand experience of pagan life in Nigeria had showed me that most of the most delightful parts of English life were really owed, all unknowingly, to Christianity. I thought that this did not necessarily mean that Christian dogma, as historically formulated, was literally, as distinct from metaphorically or symbolically, true. But it did convince me that the traditional framework of religion in England had a more absolute validity than I had previously supposed.

The family refused to allow us to go back to Nigeria but I accepted the decision without protest and decided to read theology with a view, if possible, to offering myself for Orders in the Church of England.

Lord Buckmaster asked the Archbishop of Canterbury
to give me an interview. The old Palace of Lambeth was
then, of course, undamaged and the Archbishop, Randall
Davidson, ruled from within it by means which the
rank and file of the Anglo-Catholic party regarded as
devious, even Machiavellian. I rather timidly stated
that I belonged, if anything, to that wing of the organization. The Archbishop pressed a bell and consigned me
without more ado to Cheshunt Theological College, no
doubt satisfied that such a muscular institution would iron
out any little foibles I might entertain in my fancy in that
direction. I forget how it was, but I was finally entered
at Westcott House, Cambridge. Barbara and I were
delighted, not, of course, by the tone of the college,
which was reported to be "central", but because it was
in Cambridge. We were going to have the privilege of
having lived and worked in both the old university
towns in England. To those who know about it, Cambridge had another very great attraction—it was only
about thirty miles from Thaxted in Essex. Barbara
agreed to come with me and we settled down into a little
house in Little Saint Mary's Lane, looking full south into
the sunlight, over the old garden of Little Saint Mary's
Church, and on to the lovely walls of Peterhouse.

CHAPTER THIRTEEN

THE CARDIFF MUNICIPAL MORTUARY

"Abscondisti haec a sapientibus"
Matt. II

In writing of these adventures with mines, I feel a constant regret that the cases I describe are merely those with which I was personally associated. The most spectacular cases were dealt with by other officers. If Harold Newgass could agree to write the story of the mine in the Garston Gasholder at Liverpool, or Oliver Gidden that of the other he found partly molten and fused in one piece with the live line of the electric railway on Charing Cross Bridge, or another of the party the tale of the mine with a selenium cell, my stories would hardly command a hearing. Yet no one can tell exactly what another has had to do and if what I have to write is of interest, I believe it will be so because it is written from memory.

In one way, I did quite shortly become involved at first hand with mines which were actually dismantled by other officers. In the early days, when the mines were all either concentrated in London itself, or scattered over the countryside of East Anglia, we worked alone, directed by Captain Currey from the Admiralty. In November and December of 1940, however, and in

January of 1941, mines were used by the Germans in the big raids on Coventry, Birmingham and Cardiff. To deal with the situation in these cities it was considered advisable to introduce some devolution of command. We had instant priority on the telephone, and could ring up to report, or to ask for advice from anywhere in the British Isles without a moment's delay; but in Coventry, for example, the telephone exchange was itself hit and no message could be passed to London from anywhere nearer than Leamington. In each of these raids, and in others later like them, a party of about ten officers, each with his own car, driver, sailor and kit, was dispatched from the Admiralty under the command of another whose duty was to receive the police reports on arrival, to assign a programme to each officer, arrange accommodation for the nights, to advise if required, to establish a line of communication with London if possible, and if not, to take responsibility for any decisions which must involve exceptional risk to life or property. In such a capacity it fell to me to lead a party to Coventry, to Birmingham and to Cardiff, the most familiar places of my life before the war: also, in April of 1941, to Belfast.

The raid on Coventry has been much described; from our point of view perhaps all that need be said is that Coventry was particularly difficult to work in—large parts of the centre of the city were still burning when we reached it with the following morning's daylight, and the smoke stung our eyes so that we could hardly see for tears.

The expedition to Birmingham had some entertaining features; one of the party had to dive into a canal and another officer complained that he had been compelled to remove a detached woman's leg from his mine before he could start to work on it.

Very amusing tales can be told of Belfast. But if I select Cardiff, it is because that week was associated with more laughable adventures than most others, and in particular with the case of the Cardiff Municipal Mortuary.

We always knew, not later than about eleven at night, whether a heavy raid was to be expected. On these occasions, the Germans flew their aircraft in on two converging radar beams, which were arranged to cross at the point where the bombs were to be dropped. This crossing could be detected by instruments this side of the Channel and shortly after eleven we were usually on our way, even if not a single bomb had yet fallen. That night in January, 1941, it was exceedingly cold. The Cotswolds were under snow, and when we reached Cardiff the frost was so heavy that the fire hoses froze solid in the gutters if the pumps were stopped. Accommodation, as usual, was impossible to obtain. All the remaining hotels were crammed. The police reserved us beds in Newport. I arranged the best programme I could and had settled down in my temporary office to make notes for a first report to London when a deputation was announced from the Cardiff Brewery. It was headed by the Chairman of the Board.

"I do not know whether you are aware of it, sir,"

said the Chairman with some solemnity, "but by your orders my brewery has been evacuated. The brew happens just to be coming to the boil and unless these orders can be countermanded, the Company will suffer a loss of some £1,200."

I walked across to the six-inch map on the wall of the office and indicated the position. A mine had fallen outside the main gate of the brewery and it was obvious that if it blew up under treatment, serious damage would result, with probable loss of life, unless all premises in the immediate surroundings were kept empty. I could only say that a first-class officer had been entrusted with that particular assignment, and that we would allow everybody back at the earliest possible moment, if Fortune favoured us. With that, the deputation had to be content, and withdrew. A few minutes afterwards in came Reid, the officer in question, an Australian, of great ability and courage. He said he would appreciate a second opinion on this brewery mine which presented a number of problems.

I drove down with him from the Town Hall as far as the railway line. Here, a rope had been stretched across the street by the police, just short of the railway bridge, between two Belisha beacons. "It's not much good, that rope," said Reid, "though it did wring the neck of one fellow who tried to rush the barrier on a bicycle." We left the car and walked over the granite sets towards the brewery entrance. With a movement of his left hand Reid indicated the mine. I saw with a shock that it was broken open. As was often the case, anti-aircraft fire had shot away the parachute, and the mine had fallen heavily, striking a building as it reached the ground and smashing its way into the pavement, close at the foot of the wall. Unfortunately, a water-main ran below the pavement at that point, the mine had smashed the pipe and water was welling and bubbling up all round it. Altogether, it was as nasty a case as could easily be found in the open. It could only have been worse if it had been thirty feet down below the surface. I glanced up to complete my survey of the situation, and saw that the mine was lying at the foot of a building which resembled in design a borough elementary school of the grimmer type in a back street in one of the Welsh mining valleys. Across the front of the building was carved the following legend:—

CARDIFF MUNICIPAL MORTUARY

Pinned to a door at the end on the right was a card. It read:—

"Please take bodies to. . . ."

Signed . . . Superintendent.

Reid and I grinned. The omens were propitious, and I left him after a brief discussion.

I went down again later just to see if there was anything he wanted. He had stopped the water and we were bending over the carcase of the mine in conversation when we heard heavy footsteps behind our backs.

Someone was actually walking past us, between the mortuary and the railway embankment. This was infuriating. Apart from the fact that absolute silence was required for the work, the individual would be completely destroyed, with us, if the mine suddenly went up. It also meant that efficiency had not even yet been established at the police barrier. We got up stiffly and accosted the intruder. "Don't you know," we said, "this area is evacuated by police order? You can't walk about in here; get out at once."

"I know, Guv'nor," he said, "but it's the 'orses."

"The horses!" we cried, "what on earth do you mean?" We had visions of a troop of horses cantering by over the granite.

"Yes, Guv'nor, it's the 'orses; it's time for their tea." It turned out that when the brewery had been evacuated the horses had been left in the stables.

"Why didn't you take them away?" I asked angrily.

"Nowhere to put 'em, Guv'nor."

"Nowhere to put them!" I cried, waving my hand towards the almost limitless expanse of the Cardiff marshes.

"Ain't no fence, Guv'nor," he answered.

The case was hopeless. We downed tools and followed him across the road into the brewery. There, in a long stable against the wall on the left, was a set of some twenty of the most magnificent dray horses I had ever seen.

When tea had been administered Reid returned to the

mine and his efforts in the end fortunately were successful. We were later informed that the brew was saved, but I never heard that Reid was offered any of it.

From Cardiff, I think it was, I feel forced to quote a story told, I believe, by Sam Fenwick; it is not in all respects suitable for publication and I am unable to vouch for its truth though I can assert that it is technically possible. Sam Fenwick or another officer—anyhow Sam was present either in an executive or an advisory capacity —was asked to deal with a mine which was down in the playground of one of the borough elementary schools. The two officers had located the mine and were standing at a safe distance but in full view of the weapon, blowing on their fingers, and discussing how best to set about the task of dismantling it, when a small fox terrier came on to the tarmac, trotted up to the mine and lifted its leg against the nose. In a few seconds there was a terrific explosion and the mine blew up with the usual resultant damage. The only possible explanation was that the fuse had been frozen into immobility by the cold and the little dog's contribution to the situation had melted and freed it.

Cardiff took a week. Among other things it provided me with the only mine I ever attempted after dark. It was down in Lord Bute's park, near the headquarters of the balloon barrage. It seemed necessary to clear it as soon as possible, as it was more than probable that there would be another raid on the city, perhaps that very night. I was also anxious to do what I could to save the fine old place from damage. However, my purpose is to pass on the story of the Molotov Bread Basket.

We had finished some twenty mines and had cleared the police list, so we went round to take our leave and to thank the heads of the various organizations concerned— the Lord Mayor, the chairman of the A.R.P. Committee and the Chief Constable—before going back to London. The Chief Constable was a character and maintained at his headquarters a collection of criminal exhibits, forging instruments, burglar's tools, murderer's weapons and a remarkable set of photographs taken at scenes of suicide, horror and crime. He conducted us round these exhibits and finished by saying, "Before you go, have any of you gentlemen seen a Molotov Bread Basket? I've got one down at Llandaff and have given orders to have it brought in here to-morrow morning." A Molotov Bread Basket was an arrangement for dropping clusters of fire-bombs from an aeroplane.

Travelling about the country on mining assignments, one was often asked for advice on unidentified objects which were found lying about after raids and were suspected of being dangerous. I had never seen a Molotov Bread Basket and was glad of the chance to add to my knowledge, so we stepped into a police car and drove off to Llandaff. The policeman ushered us into the front garden of a small semi-detached villa, one of a delightful little circle, with white walls and green tiled roofs. Under the porch, a baby was asleep in a pram.

The policeman waved his hand towards the rosebed

which edged the path. There, at full length, almost entirely buried in the soil, was lying one of the largest types of magnetic mine, badly damaged and in an exceedingly dangerous condition.

We had everybody out from all the houses at once.

Unfortunately, the fuse was underneath the mine and I had to make one of the cold-blooded calculations which are so common on these occasions. The houses, though charming, were worth perhaps £1,500 each and if they were completely destroyed no harm would be done to the war effort. The mine, I could see, was a standard type and was not likely to yield any secrets. In other words, it was a case, in the jargon of the Service, where "damage could be accepted".

It would be possible to request one of my officers to dig a hole under the mine, crawl in, and work on it from underneath. Alternatively, I could call up a boiler and a steam hose, and request my friend to stand over the mine and dissolve the explosive filling with steam, till so little was left that if it did go up nobody would lose anything but a few windows. But either method was so dangerous that it would only have been justified if the mine had been lying in a vital spot, a power house, an important telephone exchange, a water works, or something of that sort. I decided to trust to luck and an ordinary municipal steamroller.

It is a cardinal principle of mining that you should carry out every possible process from a distance of two hundred yards, under cover. Certain operations have to be performed actually straddling the mine, and these cannot be avoided, but there is a surprising amount that can be done at the end of a two hundred yard line. My plan of action was to make fast one end of a wire cable to a projection on the mine and the other to a steam roller, and then very gently back the roller down the hill, heave the mine out of its hole and expose the fuse for attention. The joy about these operations is that everybody is keen to help, everybody wants the mine cleared, and I have never asked in vain for any piece of apparatus which was needed, however bizarre. The answer was always "Yes". A steam roller was immediately produced; there was an excellent driver in charge, who grasped perfectly what he had to do and quite understood that there must be absolutely no jerk at any stage of the proceedings. We made fast the wire, took cover in a position from which we could watch and signalled the driver to let his roller slide slowly down the hill. The wire took the strain sweetly, the huge bulk of the mine heaved slowly up out of the rosebed; when suddenly there was an appalling explosion.

When the dust subsided, there was practically nothing left of the circle of houses. The curious thing was that the people were angry. They said that the thing had been lying there a week and if we had only left it alone, they would never have lost their property.

CHAPTER FOURTEEN

MOWBRAY'S CHURCH GUIDE, AND A PILGRIMAGE TO SHREWSBURY

"Melior est dies una in atriis tuis super millia"
· Ps. 83

In writing about the next phase, I propose to write as far as possible by implication only, and to say no more than enough to indicate the course of what followed.

Anglo-Catholicism is a fascinating province of the English mind, but I acknowledge that it cannot be interesting to everybody.

We moved to Cambridge in the autumn of 1928, and lost no time in paying a visit to Thaxted. There were those, in England then, who would never go anywhere without a copy of Mowbray's Church Guide in their pockets. This little guide listed alphabetically every Anglican church in the country where a Communion service was held on Sundays. After each name there might follow any one or more, of a selection of five different types of asterisk. Happy was the church whose name carried every one of the five : in such you would find, not only a *daily* Communion service, but also Benediction (known normally by the more discreet name of Devotions), Reservation of the Blessed Sacrament, regular times for confessions and, as a finishing touch, there would be holy water in the stoup by the door. These things, it was recognized, were nothing more than the tools of prayer; but what a joy it could be to have them. Few things, however, go perfectly smoothly in this life and there were snags which the asterisks were not designed to reveal. There were two schools of thought in the extreme reaches of Anglo-Catholicism: there was the party which pressed for an "English" form of worship and for "English" accessories, and the party which preferred a "Roman" use. The first was itself much split up into warring factions. It was bitterly disappointing to arrive at a five-star village, after perhaps a long, exhausting and expensive journey, only to find that the incumbent after all held a different school of thought from your own. A man might wear at the altar either a long wide, flowing chasuble, the English type, or a miserable little scrap of a Roman fiddle-back. He might stick to the standard Anglican prayer-book (unenterprising fellows, these) or he might have resurrected a "Sarum" form from some publication of the Alcuin club. He might read an English translation of the Roman Mass or, better still, he might read the Roman Mass itself, in the original Latin, without the omission of a syllable. He might have six candles in a row on a shelf behind the altar, or two only, standing upon the altar itself. His book might be placed upon a cushion, or upon a nasty little wood or metal framework. He might read the service audibly or *sotto voce*. The *sotto voce* might be delicate, genuinely mystical; or a discourteous, meaningless gabble. The altar might be of stone (preferably an original stone altar from the nearest ruined abbey) or wood with a small consecrated slab of white marble let into the top of it. (The stone altar, of course, would have been lying in the local farmyard for the last four centuries as a stand for slop pails or milking buckets.) The colour of the vestments, in Lent or Advent, might be rose or merely violet. The arms of the cross outlined upon the vestment might go straight across the back (a paltry type of arrangement this, worthy only of mass-producing ecclesiastical outfitters) or they might rise upwards in a shallow vee from a point in the middle of the celebrant's back and cross over his shoulders. The boy serving at the altar might be dressed in his ordinary day clothes; or a short lace cotta with his flannels showing through; or a long white surplice; or a short cotta, non-transparent, without lace; or either with a frilly collar.

You might be communicated in one kind alone or in both. You might take the Bread into your hands or (much nicer) straight into your mouth. There might be a houselling cloth along the Communion rails (old English) or you might be handed a brass dish to hold under your chin (Rome, after the issue of some instructions some time thein nineteen-thirties). All the more definitely horrid alternatives were Roman.

These things all gave great excitement and the initiated could usually judge exactly what he or she was likely to have to put up with, merely by putting a nose inside the door of a church when nothing whatever was going on there. The arrangement of the altar and credence table, the type of marker in the Bible on the lectern, would give the whole position away immediately. It was some time before I could carry out with certainty even quite a general diagnosis, and I greatly irritated my wife by inquiring one day in Saint Olave's Church in Exeter whether this was a "high" church or a "low" one. In actual fact, it was Good Friday and the altars had been stripped to the wood and duly washed with whatever is prescribed for this purpose. It accordingly looked like a "low" church, but I did not know the ritual for Holy Week, indeed I never fully learned it and, in any case, I had failed to note in the darkness that there was a crucifix behind the altar. That it was completely done up in violet chiffon did make it rather difficult to see, but that in itself should have revealed the state of affairs to me in an instant. These violet chiffon wrappings are used in only one week of the year, and only then in the very "highest" churches.

Externals must always have a great importance in religion. Did not Pugin himself point one day to a vestment and ask "How can you expect to convert England if you use a cope like that?" Unfortunately, the wrong kind of externals were so irritating to some that these people were physically unable to attend a service at all in a church where the balance at least was not on the right side. Personally, I enormously enjoyed the whole thing, but I was so aggravated by excessive sensitivity in matters of religion that I used sometimes deliberately to eat a hearty breakfast of bacon and eggs before going out to early Communion. This was an outrage of the first water, but I knew that no objection could be pressed against me. The formularies of the Anglican Church did not officially require that Communion should be taken fasting: and did not my own beloved mother follow the appalling practice of taking evening Communion at the church of Saint James in Exeter? Besides, I was a rate-payer, and as such could have put a parson into court if he had repelled me from Communion on grounds like these. I felt pretty sure what would be the verdict of the court in such a case and I was, at heart, like nearly all the English, a thorough-going Erastian.

When I later became a Roman Catholic, Barbara and I found ourselves in a bad way. There were only two, out of all the five or six thousand villages in England where there was within reach at one and the same time, a Roman Catholic chapel and a five-star Anglican church. One of them was Buckland, near Oxford, and the other was at Findon, in Sussex, and neither church was any good at all to Barbara. But those days were fortunately not yet. Thaxted, meanwhile, was perfection for both of us.

What lay at the back of all these extraordinary controversies was the fact that we were taking the first steps in prayer. I used to slip into Little Saint Mary's for some time on most days when we were in Cambridge. Saint Peter of Alcantaar says somewhere "My secret to myself" and I do not propose to write more than is strictly necessary about mine. I think it can be safely assumed that God has one for each one of us. But just a few sentences must be written about Thaxted. Those who wish can go there themselves to-day and still see much of what we saw. The living—that is, the power of presenting a clergyman for appointment—belonged then to the Countess of Warwick, and she had presented the Rev. Conrad Noel, who came to be known as the Communist Vicar of Thaxted. He was not a Communist, at any rate in the sense of being an agent in this country of the Russian revolutionary government; he was an English aristocrat, one of the Noels, Earls of Gainsborough, and he had come to the very shocking conclusion that we should all be well advised to love our neighbour to something approaching the degree to which we loved ourselves and, added to this, he thought sacraments a valuable part of the machinery of religion, he required plain dealing, he insisted that things should be beautiful, both in his own house and in God's, he had a wife with a genius for colour and form and a son-in-law who shared his views and who was also a fine musician with great talent for encouraging others to play all kinds of musical instruments. The church itself was a marvellous building, flooded with light, its walls nearly solid glass. The result of these component forces was Thaxted. The general lay-out of the services was "English", the accompaniment at the main services was orchestral, indeed the Roman party said it was a musical comedy. Being an honest man,

Noel had put the prayers in the Communion service back into their proper order, out of which they had been twisted by the Reformers, and, being an artist, he used to slip the "proper" in between the prayers, little mystical sentences from the Psalms, specially laid down for each day. In his case, I think he took the proper from the Sarum missal but I never bothered to ask; what I liked was the sentences themselves and I didn't much mind where they came from. Daily Mass at Thaxted was the perfection of public worship and nowhere will anything more lovely be seen, or heard, again. Barbara and I went there for our honeymoon at Christmas, 1926, and as often as ever we could thereafter.

Westcott House was great fun and they taught us Church History with great honesty. Unfortunately there were other candours; the Principal, Canon B. K. Cunningham, was very deaf, but the students insisted on making their confessions to him, B. K. used to sit in his study with the windows wide open and the most electrifying disclosures were bawled daily into the quadrangle.

Lord Buckmaster was standing one day in his library in London when he pulled out a book from one of the shelves and said, "Here, John, take a look at this. You write quite a good letter, but this is perfect English prose". The book was a small reddish-brown copy of Cardinal Newman's *Apologia*. I read that book and was fascinated. (It is the story of the Cardinal's conversion from the Church of England to the Church of Rome.) Anglo-Catholicism, taken theoretically, particularly the doctrine of the Apostolic Succession, was bound in any case to raise in my mind the question of the Roman claims. My upbringing at home, at school and in the wider world of Oxford, had suggested to me that Roman Catholicism was misguided, distasteful and disastrous, but clearly after all, there were great advantages on both sides; to an unprejudiced man there seemed to be wrong on both sides as well, but Roman controversialists for their part would not admit it. Had their claim to be accepted? Once the idea had entered my mind, the tormenting question for me became "Which Church is right?" The trouble with Roman Catholicism is basically that it accepts the Incarnation and only secondly that it demands a belief in the Infallibility of the Pope. But Infallibility is the more usual point of controversy. Oddly enough it was Conrad Noel, bitterly anti-Papal as he was, who made it possible for me to accept the latter. Perhaps nothing in this world is more important than that one should go to original sources—whether they are books, places, objects or people—and Conrad lent me the actual text of the Vatican Council decree on the subject of Infallibility. There I saw, with growing astonishment, that all we were required to accept in that matter was that the Pope, when speaking officially as head of the Church, would be endowed "with that infallibility which Christ wished should remain in his Church". *"Ea infallibilitate"*—not infallibility pure and simple; the decree threw the real interpretation of these words back on to the mind of Christ; whatever *he* had meant, whatever type or degree of "not failing" he had had in mind, *that* only we must assume would be granted. This might surely allow an occasional margin of error? If so, we might sweep Pope Eugenius the Fourth and his rather indiscreet letter on the subject of the "porrectio instrumentorum", the Nag's Head Fable, and the whole of the more peddling side of the argument, into the dustbin.

If the doctrine of the Incarnation were true—which was the major premiss—then there could be no doubt that unity, subject only to truth, was a first essential among Christians. The official reason for splitting the Church of England from the Church of Rome was that the Roman Catholics were in gross error, but nevertheless insisted that their errors should be swallowed; this view had been notably reinforced of recent times by the Vatican decree on Infallibility which was supposed to have made it impossible for any thinking man to join the Roman Catholic Church. I had seen that this was not necessarily correct and I thought the time had come when old quarrels should be made up. Whether the doctrine were true or not, Roman Catholicism seemed, on balance, to offer the better religious vehicle, it preserved, and still offered to the public, the most systematic method of mystical approach to Almighty God still in operation in Western Europe and the American hemisphere, it was the largest international religious body in the West, and the organization held together administratively even across political boundaries. "Securus judicat orbis terrarum" Cardinal Newman had quoted; actually, the whole world was not in the Roman Catholic Church but within that Church one could check one's experience against the experience of a far wider selection of human beings than was possible in the Church of England. "J'aime ma propre tradition," Mrs. Ruxton used to say in Nigeria; it seemed clear that provided one kept a rather wary eye open the soundest course was to take Roman Catholicism with a pinch of salt (as indeed is necessary with everything else), and make the best use possible of such religious apparatus as was available.

This was certainly going rather far in the direction of liberalism in religious matters. I consulted as many people as I could about this, but none found really important the issues which took up my own attention, except for Dr. Gamble, then Dean of Exeter. In his lovely upstairs study in the Deanery, he gravely heard me out. "My dear John," he said at length, "if you leave the Church of England for the Church of Rome you will find that you will be exchanging one set of problems for another." In due course this turned out to be quite correct, but what matters is which set of problems you find tolerable. The value of his remark to me at that stage was that he had not rejected the Roman Church out of hand; he was clearly of the opinion that the two organizations, Rome and Canterbury, could be weighed one against the other as alternatives, of at least something like the same order of value: other people always threw up their hands in horror, either at one or at the other. Everything was either black or white with them.

A decision of some kind was clearly necessary if only as a matter of practical politics. I could not either go forward to Orders in the Church of England, or become a Roman Catholic, until I had hammered one out. I went away to Overy Staithe again, determined to do my utmost to reach a conclusion. I walked some way out into the marshes; the larks were up; the sun was out, though rather misted, the air was glorious, the solitude was absolute. I threw myself down on the grass on the side of a bank and implored God to help me. I decided to address the Holy Ghost for a change; I had been reading Fr. Baker's book on the Holy Wisdom and felt rather ashamed that I had never yet approached the Almighty except as God the Father. The reply came with startling suddenness; it was devoid of any introduction or trimmings; it was like a clap of thunder.

"They are both wrong."

In a few moments I was laughing. The point was, of course, not that both must be held to be actually misleading, but that some discount should be applied to some of the assertions put forward by protagonists on both sides. I saw that I need not really take the controversy so desperately seriously. The thing about God's remarks is that they do always settle an argument. Difficulties in coming to a decision are so often due to a failure to take into consideration some point or aspect which may really control the whole situation. The

XIXth Article of the Church of England states that the Church of Rome hath erred. It was delicious to discover that God heartily agreed with my fellow-Anglicans. My mind was steeped in the language of centuries and I had really thought it probable that the Almighty would be found to be definitely on one side or the other; it was a blessed relief to find Him so caustically neutral.

I was still left with the decision to make for myself but now felt free to decide it upon the general grounds which I have described.

The question may be asked how ever I got myself accepted by a Catholic priest. It was done in perfect innocence. I was staying in Shropshire and went to Shrewsbury and rang the bell at the Presbytery. Canon A. J. Moriarty (later Bishop of Shrewsbury) opened the door. I hadn't the least idea who he was, but saw he was a responsible man and no doubt busy; I did not want to bother him with all my troubles—I simply said I wanted to become a Catholic. "Why?" said the Canon, with his hand still on the door-knob. I was dealing with an official, of course (though one who, I saw, had a twinkle in his eye) so I suppose by instinct I elected to start my answer to so colossal a question by taking an administrative point. "I am a student at an Anglican theological college," I replied, "and I have come to the conclusion that the Pope ought to be acknowledged as the head of the church." "Come in," said the Canon, and as far as I remember there was no further conversation on controversial subjects.

CHAPTER FIFTEEN

BUSMAN'S HOLIDAY

"Numquid omnes Apostoli?"
1 Cor. 12

In the Admiralty records, I am myself credited with having tackled personally only fifteen mines. An idea of the part played by other members of the squad can be gathered from the bald statement that Ronnie Forrt dismantled forty-six. One officer, who had perhaps better be nameless, carried out so heavy a programme that he fell deeply into debt. This must sound like a *non-sequitur*, for obviously no man could drink to excess, or otherwise degenerate into vices, and at the same time continue with such work, but in actual fact, nobody could remain in the party unless he had private means; in that respect the State resembled that of Holy Orders in the Church of England. The explanation was that wherever we went the place was *ex hypothesi* blitzed to the ground, accommodation either did not exist or was extremely expensive, it was winter-time and impossible to sleep in tents, even if there had been time to cook food, each officer had with him a sailor and an Army driver, these men received an allowance of about three shillings and sixpence a day, they shared our dangers, and at the end of a nerve-wracking and exhausting assignment, on which one had invariably worked into the first darkness, often cold and sometimes wet, it would have been impossible to say to these men "Dis-miss! Parade 06.00 to-morrow". The only thing to do in practice was to take the men into one's own hotel and pay the bill. All of us have recollections of the greatest kindnesses; people of all ranks welcomed us into their houses in case of need, impartially—I would like to thank especially the householders of Leamington who took us in for the whole period of the operations in Coventry and refused to charge a penny. But more often than not, the only practicable course was to make for some hotel, and pay.

On the only occasion on which Saint John the Baptist is reported to have addressed the armed forces as such, the only instruction he gave them was that they were to be content with their wages. But the fact was that we received no pay or allowances for the whole of the first three months. When at last we had time and strength to investigate the matter (none of us knew, of course, what were the rates of naval pay or the regulations governing subsistence allowance) we discovered that the trouble had been that nobody could decide what "ship's books" we were on; were we to be carried on the account of H.M.S. *Vernon*, in Portsmouth, or were we to be debited to H.M.S. *President*, the titular ship of the Admiralty? Old hands, in such circumstances, would have had no difficulty, they would merely have drawn an advance, but we did not know that there was provision of that kind under the King's Regulations. The time came, about

Christmas, 1940, when the pile of hotel bills due from this particular officer grew rather heavy—they were lying about all over the room upstairs in Bank Block. We acquired a copy of King's Regulations and put our heads together. On a certain page we discovered a table of Colonial Allowances. Running down the list of stations, we noticed that an officer posted in Mesopotamia drew a very handsome allowance indeed. I took a pen and wrote a minute to the effect that it was of considerable importance, from information received, that an officer of our party should be sent to take charge of certain investigations in the Tigris. I recommend Lieut. . . . as an officer of great experience and ability, well suited for the post, the recommendation was accepted by some portion of the Admiralty machine, and the Lieutenant disappeared overnight into comparative affluence.

Apart from the mines with which we dealt personally the senior members of the party had to instruct new recruits. There was something amusing walking round a mine with a newcomer, pointing gravely with a stick and saying, "If I were you, I should begin *there*", and then retiring to safety a hundred yards away, though, of course, one was sorry for anyone who was tackling a mine for the first time and could not help being anxious, even if the indications were that things ought to go according to plan. We regarded these expeditions—and certain others—as a form of holiday, and if we were tired, or out of sorts, would volunteer for them. On one such occasion I drove north to Mansfield with a raw recruit. We located our objective early on a Sunday afternoon; it was lying out on rough land on a considerable slope, at the back of a housing estate. The green parachute showed up clearly across the valley. It was a sunny day and I noted with pleasure that a little hedge ran diagonally across the hill, about thirty yards below the mine; a hedge provides excellent protection against blast and there were prospects that if trouble arose my friend could escape serious injury to his lungs, at any rate, if he could once put that hedge between himself and an explosion. We walked cautiously round the mine; there were indications that it was of a standard design and the early stages of the operation were not obstructed so, after making a few suggestions, I retired to the rather risky distance of about seventy yards and lay down in a shallow depression in the ground. I did not put more between us, because for some indefinable reason I felt anxious and I wanted to be able to talk to B in case of need. Hardly had he put a hand on the mine when from a corner behind the nearest houses there arose the strains of the hymn, "*Eternal Father: strong to save.*" The excellent commander of the local Salvation Army contingent had observed our plight, had seen that we were in naval uniform, and had instructed his band to address the Almighty in our interests, in the obvious medium. Poor B, badly baulked, and quite unable to hear whatever might be going on inside the mine, downed tools and fled.

When quiet was restored—I must say the band took

my explanations with the readiest and most affectionate sympathy—B gallantly returned to his work; when suddenly I saw him drop everything and start to run. Hardly had he reached the hedge when there was the usual terrific explosion. Seeing that B was going to be more or less all right, I was about to shout some friendly gibe when my blood began to feel cold. Rock and stones were falling all round me out of the sky. They were returning to earth from the crater formed by the explosion. I cursed myself for an idiot; after all these adventures had I put myself in a position to be killed by a rock falling on my head or back? I clasped my arms over my head and hoped for the best. Nothing hit me; B seemed to be unhurt, though naturally much shaken and a little affected in the lungs, so I suggested adjourning for a "holiday" in Norfolk.

The mine I proposed to look at proved also to be on open ground. Weapons of that character were common at the time so there was no real need to risk life in an attempt to take it to pieces. The easiest and safest thing to do was to blow it up with a charge of gun-cotton. The only objection to that course was that it would leave behind an enormous crater and unless the farmer happened to want a pond in that position we should be considered thoughtless. It was also possible to remove a cover plate and set fire to the explosive filling and let it burn itself away. It would burn with a magnificent shower of silver sparks. If the primers had been removed, the probabilities were that the filling would burn itself out without an explosion. The method was to pile some paper and a few dry sticks against the exposed part of the filling, set a match to the outside edge of the pile, and dash off, just in case of accidents. B was feeling better and volunteered to remove the primers. This was safely accomplished and we staged our little show, collected the village school-children, ranged them carefully in a ditch from which they could see the fun without serious danger, and set fire to the filling. The mine burned beautifully, rounding off the display with a little final explosion.

From there we separated, and I drove down to the charming village of Stoke-by-Clare, on the borders of Suffolk and Essex. In a window in the south aisle of Thaxted Church is a stained glass figure of a Prior of Stoke-by-Clare and in another are the arms of Gilbert de Clare once, long ago, Earl of Gloucester. Often and often I had gazed at these windows as I listened to Conrad Noel, or Jack Puttrill, saying the morning Mass in the lovely Thaxted liturgy. My information was that there was now a mine on a farm on the outskirts of the village.

It was a Wednesday and I called at the police station about mid-day to ask for a guide. The Sergeant in charge came out, obviously straight from his dinner and not perhaps best pleased at being disturbed. I explained my errand. It should be remembered that these mines were sea-mines, designed to be dropped in harbours and their approaches, and would remain in perfect order, under water, for a period of at least three years. The following dialogue took place.

"Oh," said the Sergeant, "I don't think you need worry much about that one, sir".

"Why, Sergeant, has it gone off?"

"No, sir, and it won't either." I looked at him in surprise; was it possible that this man was something of an expert?

"No, sir; it fell on Monday and we've had a bit of rain since then."

Many other ridiculous stories there are in my memory. One was the case of the mine near Watton in Norfolk. It was a lovely afternoon in late autumn as my sailor and I reached the spot. The mine was down in an open copse among bracken and brambles on a part of a great estate. A pale golden sunlight gilded the dry grass, pheasants were calling, we seemed very far from the troubles of the world. The mine, again of a standard pattern, was dangling by its parachute from a young oak. There was no reason why it should not be cleared by straightforward demolition, the copse would confine the blast and little serious damage would be done. But it would be easier if the thing was on the ground. We made a long cable fast to a convenient length of the parachute cords, retired to the end of it and from there dragged and shook the mine down. If it went up under this treatment so much the better. It fell with a dunt, rolled a turn or two and came to rest. We lay flat for two minutes to give it time to explode if it wished to do so. Nothing happened.

My sailor turned a red face in my direction. On this particular afternoon it was not Tuckwell, but the name shall not be given as I am about to relate a breach of Admiralty orders.

"I wonder, sir," he said, "do you think I might do this mine?"

There was no pressing reason why he should do it; indeed, there were several why he should not; but there seem to come times in life when disobedience has a value. At any rate it occurs. I nodded.

He took the tools and went forward. Following the ordinary routine, I lay flat and watched. He sat astride the carcase and got to work on the first ring. In a few moments he dropped the spanner, leapt into the air and started running as fast as he could towards me. Stumbling and falling as the brambles caught his legs, he finally managed to reach my lair and flung himself on the ground, panting. I shrank down as low as I could and waited. No explosion.

When he had got some of his breath back I said, "What happened?" "Oh, sir," he gasped, "it's a-groaning on me!" I burst into laughter. These mines frequently had differential pressures inside them and at certain stages they would groan like a dying animal. I had forgotten to tell him.

To his credit he got up at once, walked back to the mine and finished the job.

It can help a great deal—for instance, thirty or forty feet down under Thames mud—if one's sailor knows what has to be done. But it is not in the book of rules.

CHAPTER SIXTEEN

THE RELIGION OF SAINT JAMES
1930-39

"Religio immunda et immaculata apud Deum et Patrem est haec:"
Jac. I

All through the time at Cambridge I had hanging over me the cloud which had descended so catastrophically in the autumn of 1925, more than three years before. In March of this year, 1929, I temporarily collapsed. It came upon me that it was absolutely impossible in England, as it was then, consistently to follow out the advice to love one's neighbour as oneself. It was impossible to avoid, in the ordinary course of events, using equipment for example which had been made in conditions which one would not willingly tolerate for oneself—if it were only a kitchen stove cast in some factory in the Black Country, where men might be paid, indeed, a living wage but had to live in hideous circumstances. Far worse than this, if the term neighbour included other forms of life which had evolved in parallel with us upon this planet, it was impossible to eat; or even to walk across a field without crushing blades of grass in thousands. My father and mother took me down to Dartmoor and we stayed in the Two Bridges Hotel.

Here I came to two conclusions: first, as regards human beings, that the only thing to do was to do one's best in ordinary life and work, to improve the existing social framework to a point where it could become the framework of a co-operative, not a repressive society; meanwhile one had to take things as one found them. As regards the other and really more difficult point, it was surely clear that if there were a God, then it could only be He who had laid down these uncompromising principles, eating and walking, as an inescapable part of human life; if so, He must have had His own reasons for it, which either I should, or should not, in due course, come to appreciate. In either case, the only sensible thing to do was to cheer up and go back to London.

This was, of course, an extreme example of a trouble which was to beset me for many years, the sense of an inescapable incompatibility between much of a normal human existence and a state of conversation with Almighty God or, as it were, of "living the next life now".

In 1939, I became so wearied with it that I begged Almighty God to clear it up for me.

I was kneeling in the early morning in my lovely great bedroom in Northamptonshire; through the three tall windows and the hanging tendrils of the montana creeper in full flower, the light was flooding in from the east garden; when the Lord suddenly remarked, "If you will do My Will, you will find this life in perfect harmony with the next". I do not know why, and I am more than doubtful whether I have done his Will since then, even in the more important respects, but somehow I have never again found myself worried about this.

Once freed, if only in large part, from this frightful incubus, the usual sort of whimsical considerations began to flood back into my mind—what my father used to call "High Church jokes". He began by thinking these jokes very irreverent, which indeed they are, but he came in time even to make a good number himself. In this case, I was reminded of the example of Origen's condemnation. Origen, an African, and a barrister in the early days of the Church, took seriously the first ten verses of the eighteenth chapter of St. Matthew's Gospel. It was not an eye, a hand or a tooth which was troubling Origen, but a different member, and unfortunately he had in mind another scriptural reference, St. Matthew, 19, 12, also from our Lord's reported words, which seemed to authorize what he proposed to do. He removed the member and was promptly condemned as a heretic. It seemed that here was an excellent example of the danger of acting on what looks like an indisputable interpretation of a legal directive without first consulting competent authority. In my case, I had clearly grossly over-strained the terms of the Parable of the Good Samaritan.

The principle that truth is what authority says it is, is well established in many important avenues of life. In the Admiralty for example in the war, when things really mattered, we found that there never had been at any time what might be called a platonic conception of truth. Truth was what a man said, or wrote, who had more rings round his sleeve than you had. I once went in much distress to an Admiral of great experience, with a file of papers. I had written a minute explaining in some detail why we must have a certain sum of money for a certain operational purpose. The answer came that we could not have it and I asked him what to do. He smiled gravely and dipped his pen in the ink. "This is what we will do," he said. He wrote at the bottom of the sheet the one word "Concur" and signed the minute. I looked at him astounded; he was slightly deaf, and for a moment I was afraid that he had not heard my explanation. "But, sir," I said, "we must have this money."

"My dear John," he replied, "I assure you that if you will always write 'Concur' at the foot of an Admiralty minute, it is exceedingly unlikely that you will ever be troubled with the paper again."

Unfortunately, all these salutary considerations came too late. While I had been away on Dartmoor, our first child had been born, and I had been of no use to Barbara. However, things at last began to take a turn for the better. I had spent eight years in honest efforts to unearth a ration of truth about the world. Fantastic scruples about religion and morale were being cleared up, and it seemed obvious that what was wanted in England in 1929 was that as many people as possible should be given as many chances as possible to work things out for themselves. If they could have a little more help than I had met with, it certainly would not do them any harm. In other words, the first need was for more opportunities

for education. I went off for a short holiday in South
Wales with Tony Disney, who was for ever picking me
up and dusting me. By the spring of 1931 I had become
deputy director of education in Hampshire. I was ill in
bed with influenza. I wanted to take out an insurance
policy to cover some of the expenses of educating my
children and the manager of the Clerical, Medical
Assurance Society came up from Southampton to arrange
it. He happened to be interested in Major Douglas'
Social Credit scheme, he thought it might interest me
and knowing I was in bed he kindly brought me a copy
of *This Age of Plenty*.

This was my first introduction to economics, in
particular to the theory of money. Such details had never
been discussed in my family, or in my circle at the university, nor had they been mentioned by the officials in
Nigeria, or even in the many discussions I had heard in
Lord Buckmaster's houses in London or Scotland. The
fallacy in Douglas' argument is somewhat subtle, and is
not at all easy to grasp, yet grasp it one must if one is to
understand modern currency management. I couldn't
see it myself, naturally enough, but I was for a time in
good company, including that of the Prime Minister and
Provincial Government of Alberta. I was entranced with
some of the general principles he sets out, and in many,
events have proved him to have been perfectly right
wherefore *The Age of Plenty* might well still be set as a
first text-book in economics—if it contains a "*pons asi-
norum*", so much the better.

The next discovery was the verbatim proceedings of the Macmillan Committee on Finance and Industry, which was appointed by the Labour Government in 1929. It was a large, uncomfortable volume in a blue paper cover published by His Majesty's Stationery Office at the terrific price of something like £3 12s. 6d. If it cost £350 it would be an excellent investment. The Committee hammered their way through every important branch of the financial activities of the city of London. Incidentally the proceedings show the essential greatness of Mr. Ernest Bevin. Mr. Bevin was a member of the Committee. The procedure was to summon a leading exponent of the branch of work under review, invite him to give a lecture on his subject, and then question him closely upon every point of importance in his answer. Mr. Bevin did not appear to understand by any means the whole of what was said, but he was far too big a man to sit and pretend that he did; he insisted, time and again, upon having a complex or sketchy statement repeated in simpler and clearer language, until there could be no mistake as to what was meant, and how it fitted in with the general scheme and with the statements of other witnesses. It is thanks to Mr. Bevin that the evidence is as intelligible as it is. It is true that much of the value of this evidence is the light it throws upon the working of the old Gold Standard; the Exchange Equalization Account was unfortunately still in the future; but the evidence is very valuable for all that. Illness is a great trial but I have usually found that illnesses have given me my only chances to make any serious steps forward. When the Macmillan Committee evidence was finished, I was well enough to go back to the office; but before I went I sent in a subscription to the *Economist*. I have read every issue which has appeared since and I owe more to that paper than I can possibly express.

The crux of the day in the early 1930's, it will be remembered, was unemployment. Yet the extraordinary thing was that by and large the English upper classes elected to ignore it. At tea in the Deanery, Winchester, one afternoon I was solemnly informed, though not by the Dean, that if only those wretched miners would take jobs as gardeners the matter would be finished; they were far too well off on the dole to consider honest work. In actual fact, there were at times about two million on the registers, and a man who had a wife and two children to support drew the colossal sum of twenty-seven shillings and threepence for all purposes, including house rent. The National Council of Social Service did not ignore the problem; one of its objects was to consider ways and means of improving the lot of the unemployed, it urged the formation of special clubs for them, it suggested various activities which might prove useful and possible, it collected and distributed reports on what was being done and what had been a success in different districts, and money was entrusted to it by the Government out of which it was able to back up deserving projects in the most practical of all ways. It ran a training centre (at King's Standing near Burton-on-Trent) for club leaders and members of club committees. The trouble with the National Council was that it never got down to bedrock. It went on the old English principle of the palliative. It did not dare to say that what was wanted was a means of setting the unemployed to productive work, as a means of maintenance. It concentrated instead upon a series of efforts to brighten their lives. The reason was, of course, that the possessing classes who financed it, either directly or through the Government, did not want any new production which could possibly compete with their own. Over the whole field of production private enterprise was already represented and the theory ran that what we were suffering from was "over-production". It was hard enough to sell what was already being produced, without subsidizing extra production. The average rate-paying shopkeeper and town councillor would rather the unemployed man spent his twenty-seven shillings (and threepence) in the shop in the next street, than risk making an effort to put the fellow on his feet again and turn him into a substantial customer. It was "The Age of Plenty". The ghastly irony of this view Major Douglas did his best to show up. A similar background of economic theory dominated the Government's own direct schemes for dealing with the "depressed areas". "Trading Estates" could be started, but only as a means of easing the path for some form of private enterprise. The Government did assist one practical effort, but this was possible politically because the work was on a small scale only and though it did subsidize

a form of production, it was a case of producing food-
stuffs, in the home country, for which there were
strategic arguments. This was the Land Settlement
Association. Prominent in this were L. D. Gammans,
then a wild man from Malay but later a Conservative
M.P., and Lord Phillimore, the son of the well-known
ecclesiastical lawyer. The method was to acquire agricultural properties of about five hundred acres each, keep
in hand about half the estate, with the central buildings
and split up the balance into holdings of some ten acres
each; every holding had a three-bedroomed house and
a few small outbuildings. Suitable-looking unemployed
men (with suitable-looking wives) who volunteered for
the experiment were accepted for a short period of training
and then were entrusted with a holding of their own at
a fixed rental. They had to grow what they were told to
grow, and in the way they were told to grow it; all
buying and all selling was done centrally by the central
farm; all necessary machinery was kept on the central
farm and the buildings were so arranged that the heavy
cultivation could be done centrally. The farm grew
feeding-stuffs for the holdings, and built up and maintained
stocks of pigs, poultry, young fruit-trees, tomato plants,
etc., for distribution to the holdings at the right time.
There was a managing committee of practical farmers
for each estate; many of the members were local and they
included representatives of the County agricultural staffs.
The aim was to show in a few years that estates run on
such a principle could keep their heads above water

financially, and provide the men with a living rather better than the living they had on the dole—a standard of about 52s. a week was the average target. Apart from this, the men had the advantage of an open-air life in beautiful surroundings, a decent house, and a training in agriculture.

There were, of course, heavy expenses, both capital and for maintenance at the start; these were met partly from Government grants disguised or straightforward, and partly from private sources.

One of the first of the estates was set up near St. Neots in Huntingdonshire; the intention was to try to cash in on the existing London fruit and vegetable market. I had the luck to meet Gammans early on, when I was trying to interest my own County Smallholding Committee in this scheme, and he agreed to set up an estate in my own county of Hampshire. Park Farm near Andover was chosen. The County Council, my employers, very kindly allowed me to join the managing committee and we had the good fortune to secure Lord Phillimore himself as Chairman. He was very good and took the most practical interest possible in all the work, including the siting, the design and the appearance of the small-holders' cottages. No "truth by number of rings" for him. Each estate specialized in a different type of work according to the nature of the soil and the nature of the nearest market of any size. Men from the "Depressed Areas"—later, in our mealy-mouthed way, rechristened the "Special Areas"—had first claim, but one could slip in suitable men from elsewhere in twos or threes. When it is considered that there were ten thousand unemployed upon the registers in Southampton alone—a supposedly "prosperous" area, it will be understood that we could have no illusions about the scale on which we were working. However, it was at least a start. It was odd in a way that the Government was prepared to finance these land schemes, but the conception that farming would have to be subsidized was gaining ground at the time and it was thought that farm production was therefore likely to be able to stand a little expansion. Another practical scheme was set on foot by the Society of Friends (the Quakers), who issued garden tools and seeds at subsidized prices. Peter Scott launched the Brynmawr experiment in a derelict mining town in South Wales with over 50 per cent. unemployment; he started a furniture factory with a show-room in London, and later on a small farm and other productive ventures. The furniture did quite well.

I do not want this chapter to turn into a disquisition on unemployment in Great Britain in the nineteen-thirties; but merely to do two things, first to remind my readers of the general position, and then to show the sort of thing which was attempted, how little we could do and why. We were heavily handicapped by the insanity of the economic system (but then that, of course, was responsible for the whole state of affairs). If we were to ensure any continued financial support, even for quite tiny ventures, or so much as to avoid actual hostile attack, we found in most cases that we were forced to avoid production for sale on the open market and had to limit ourselves to helping the unemployed man to produce goods for sale or distribution among his family and his unemployed friends. In other words, you could do little more than help him to get better value for his pittance of 27s. 3d. My own particular line lay in my knowledge of, and interest in, the legal powers of spending money which Parliament conferred upon local government bodies; I reported on these to the National Council of Social Service, and lectured for them at King's Standing, pointing out to representatives from all over the country what activities could be subsidized and which local government body (and which officials) should be approached in each case in the first instance. I travelled up and down England visiting centres for the unemployed, acquainting myself at first hand with the type of man out of work and the men (and women) interested in trying to tackle the problem, and served as a member of the committee of the big club for unemployed men in Southampton docks. I also acted as secretary to a group of education officers from the counties and county boroughs who met once a quarter to discuss administrative problems and any new educational legislation; the leading spirits were Sir Henry Morris, of Cambridgeshire, R. Y. Logan, later director of education in Lincolnshire and Worcestershire, Robert Beloe, chief education officer in Surrey, and W. E. Philip, now secretary to the County Education Committee in Devon. All this was quite outside my full-time office duties and was mostly done at week-ends; I managed somehow to get in a good deal of yachting in and around the Solent and some riding, and I slipped abroad at times. I was young and strong, we had a very substantial private income and my official work, though tiring, was entirely congenial and in Peter Coates I had the most delightful, kind, shrewd master. Nevertheless, the pace was too hot.

England was a very strange place in the early 'thirties, and life was exceedingly difficult for anyone in the upper classes with a cross-bench mind who had happened to notice the contrast between the conditions of the well-to-do and the conditions of the poor. Difficult because it was practically impossible to continue ordinary social contacts with members of the upper classes unless one kept one's mouth shut. Either the facts were genuinely unknown (and this, I am convinced, was the more usual case) or else they were known, but deliberately accepted as a necessary result of maintaining a system of private enterprise, and with it the standards of life required to produce a controlling class. Where the facts were not known, an account of them caused such a revulsion of feeling that in self-defence the hearer refused to believe them, or else maintained that the account must be greatly exaggerated. Where they were known, one came up against a flinty determination, and a broad hint that one was being disloyal to one's class and cutting at the organization of society to which was owed everything in life which was worth having. It is odd, for example, that

there was no London club for well-to-do persons interested in putting right the social and economic order.
The nearest approach was my own club, the Reform,
which was not interested in present-day reform at all, but
inherited its premises, its organization and its test of
membership from the days of the Reform Bill of a
hundred years earlier.   It was then admitted that
though in theory the club was a Liberal club, a Tory M.P.
could be elected to membership—the principles of the
Representation of the People Act, 1918, being of course
well in advance of the principle which had seemed so
liberal at the time of the Reform Bill. Even so it was,
and is, a liberal-minded club and in the war the members
were not above making the observation that the Almighty
did at least seem to prefer them to the occupants of the
Tory club next door, whose premises were so satis-
factorily destroyed by a bomb. But it was in no sense a
Socialist society.

In the course of the ten years, 1929-39, I came to
learn more and more of the real state of affairs. Among
other things, the Children and Young Persons Act of
1932 laid down that in future no case concerning a child
or young person under seventeen should come before
the courts until a report had been presented by the local
Education Authority upon the circumstances of the
child's home. This ruling applied, whether the child was
the injured party, or the alleged offender. Many of these
cases were cases of cruelty or neglect; the files were open
to my inspection and in some cases I myself made official

visits to the houses. In such instances, of course, we were dealing with conditions in comparatively favourable circumstances in the villages and small country towns which made up the administrative area of the County of Hampshire; the slums of Portsmouth and Southampton though in the geographical county, were under separate administrative control. Yet even in the country I found conditions as bad, morally and materially, as anywhere else in my experience; all that could be said was that the scale, mercifully, was smaller. The fact was that there were serious and substantial poverty and degradation in all the large centres in England and Wales (to say nothing of Scotland); but three areas in particular were singled out for some official attention, the so-called "Depressed Areas" of Tyneside, West Cumberland and South Wales. Brynmawr, where Peter Scott made his determined attack upon the roots of the problem, was at the head of one of the long, deep, mining valleys in South Wales; few Englishmen drove through those valleys—they led nowhere except to the moors and these could be reached more directly, and far more pleasantly, through Abergavenny and the charming country of Herefordshire. I had only three weeks' holiday a year but I had also the Bank Holiday week-ends, the longest of which was Easter, for it started on Good Friday. I took my eldest son to Brynmawr on Good Friday, to show him the modern crucifixion. On all these expeditions, there was much to see and find out. It is curious to recall that when I first entered an education office I was astonished to discover that the State elementary schools were "mixed" —that is, taught boys and girls together. That in itself shows to what an extraordinary degree the classes were separated in the England of my youth. Disraeli speaks in one of his nineteenth-century novels of the "Two Nations" of England; those two nations, deriving no doubt, from the Norman conquest, still lived independent lives nine hundred years later—independent save for the fact that one lived upon the back of the other. In the upper half of such a society the subject of Russia was naturally taboo and in 1935 I decided to spend my summer holiday in Russia.

I wanted to discover two things in particular, apart from gaining a general impression; I wanted to find out how the U.S.S.R. "managed" its paper currency, and how the two new types of communal agriculture worked, the so-called "State" farms and the "Collective" farms. Unless one were a diplomat one could normally go to Russia in those days only on an "Intourist", state-conducted tour, but that seemed good enough; I think it was Aristotle who said that a man's real nature was the best that he had it in him to be, and I considered that if it were true that the Russians only showed to foreigners the show pieces, well, that was precisely what must have most significance and value. As a matter of fact, this turned out to be only a canard, as I shall show. But as a beginning I went to the Intourist office in Bush House in Aldwych and explained what I wanted. I was told to go to Moscow for the finance and to the area around Rostov on the Don for the farming; was handed my tickets and was soon on my way in a British aircraft from Croydon. I had never flown before and was delighted with the Dutch airport at Amsterdam with its terrace and yellow umbrellas—as we came down there seemed to be less earth about than water, and that we must inevitably land in a canal. Berlin was a little grimmer and more what I was accustomed to, though the Continental beauty and dignity of the Adlon Hotel still remains in my memory. Most delightful of all was the airfield at Kaunas (Kovno) in the Baltic States; close green turf lapped up to a hedge of round, clipped hydrangeas in full flower along the terrace in front of the airport buildings.

But we had already touched Russia; at Dantzig, two stops further back, we had left our German plane and entered a Russian one. Painted a dirty green, tied up with wire and with the black, oily driving shaft and differential of a motor lorry stuffed along the gangway between the seats, it had struck us with a certain distaste and even alarm. In this peculiar vehicle we took off again from Kaunas and soon were actually over Russian territory. For some two hours we flew over a vast width of pine forest and black swamp, featureless except for occasional rivers dotted with logs which from a height looked like nothing so much as matchsticks spilled out of a box; this landscape finally showed signs of breaking into some cultivation, the soil turned red and we dropped towards our first Russian airfield at Velikie Lukie. To our horror, we saw that the whole field was covered with long, waving grass and dotted with heaps of gravel, old iron rails and other rubbish. Our pilot plunged resolutely into this area and deposited us safely at the buildings. These were quite new and very small—a row of hastily erected whitewashed concrete huts. I made my way to the lavatory and saw, to my intense surprise, a row of seven water-closet pedestals, complete with tank, chain and downpipe, standing against the wall, without a vestige of a partition between any of them. Several of them were in use.

Clearly we had left Europe behind for good at Kaunas. But I found affairs bracing. Had I not complained, for fifteen years, of the lack of candour in English society?

Once in the air again, I studied my Russian companions. From the fact that they were travelling by air at all, they must have occupied positions of some importance, yet there was not a grey hair in the head of any one of them. This seemed very remarkable to me; I had come to associate responsible position in England with grey hair and an invincible objection to change. We were flying over wide, rolling country, closely cultivated, the soil showing a Devonshire red. At intervals we passed over a village. I was astonished to see that most of the houses seemed to be little squat cellars of mud, with mud roofs covered with grass and weeds. In the centre of each village was a colossal church, painted white, with a large gilded dome. I began to see some point in the Bolshevik's more vitriolic references to the Orthodox Establishment.

Once in Moscow, I had a piece of luck; I fell in with a

delegate from South Africa who was visiting Russia, and seeing that I was alone he very kindly invited me to join him. The ordinary Intourist trip was so arranged that the traveller made his way—tickets and all necessary information provided—from the Intourist office in one town to the Intourist office in another. In each town on arrival, he would be assigned a "Guide", whose business it was to take him around, book his accommodation in an hotel, pay his bill, answer questions and generally look after him. Often in the larger towns, he might have to form one of quite a large party, and in such cases there might not be much chance of any extended talk with the guide, or with anyone else. When he left a town he left his guide behind him, and found quite a different one awaiting him in the next place. I think everyone who visited Russia in those days acquired the warmest respect and admiration for these guides. Always women, they were young, clever and good linguists; they were usually of university type, they were broadminded and tactful to a degree, but one and all genuinely attached to the Revolution and determined to explain, if they could, the meaning and significance of the institutions which were visited. Thus even if I had been left to follow the ordinary routine I should have been very well served; but in this case we had the great advantage that my friend had had a private guide attached to him. She went everywhere with us, throughout, arranged everything we wanted to do, and was willing to talk to us all the time and to explain everything. The *only* difficulty was one which some people may find hard to believe—the fact that Vera was determined that we should not go home and say we had been shown nothing but what the Government wanted. She carried this to a most irritating extreme. We would arrive in a town, with little time to spare, and we would ask Vera what we ought to see. "Oh, you must say what sort of thing you want to look at." One day we had tramped for hours round a tractor factory and there was only time for a short visit to the operatives' housing scheme. We asked Vera to cut things short by showing us a typical set of accommodation. "I shall do no such thing," said Vera. "You can knock at whatever door you choose," (waving her arm vaguely round an estate of about a hundred acres) "and I shan't tell you, even if I know it is only a coal-hole. All I can say is that if anyone comes out, I will deal with the situation for you."

Here was a country where facts were facts and were openly acknowledged, and what was more, where something was being done about them. The whole place was under construction. Everywhere there were signs of a certain material inefficiency—there were no plugs in the new baths, steps had disintegrated in the ferro-concrete stairways. We went round the State milk-processing factory in Rostov—a town of 250,000, about the size of Southampton. The greatest care was taken to preserve cleanliness throughout; all machinery and utensils were scrupulously scalded with steam, the workers were made to wear clean white overalls and caps and were given a manicure regularly once a week. As usual, when we were about to go, the Director asked us what we thought of his factory. We said we had been greatly impressed; but could he explain why the milk was brought in from the country in churns which were actually rusty inside? It seemed to us to make nonsense of his own rather elaborate precautions. He grinned. "Moscow," he said, "has not yet been able to supply us with new churns. But they will do so before long, and meanwhile, it does us good to practice cleanliness wherever we can." In the main square outside, workmen were standing on the spires of a church, driving their picks in between the stones and bringing the place down as quickly as was practicable.

Later that week we were driving back into Rostov from the huge State farm at Tsernograd. This covered 200,000 acres, the size of the Isle of Wight, and was farmed from a central group of high buildings, flats, workshops, offices, schools, canteens, etc., which looked for all the world like a suburb of Moscow dumped down in the countryside. The work was done by huge caterpillar tractors drawing as many as seven different implements, one behind another; the tractors were fitted with powerful lights ahead and astern, and work went on throughout the night. As we were approaching the new State Theatre in the outskirts of Rostov, a huge building in concrete and glass which has since been much shown in films abroad but was then, like nearly everything else, under construction, I noticed a solitary figure on the footpath on the right-hand side. It was dressed in an old beaver hat, once black, and a long dusty cassock. "Vera," I said with some excitement, drawing her attention to the figure. "Isn't that a priest?" She looked hard at it. "Ugh!" she said, "yes; he ought to go and do something respectable." I longed to tell this story to the County Education Committee—preferably when the Dean was present in his gaiters. But sorrowfully I realized that such a thing could not possibly be done. Or if it were done, that there would be no laughter.

Nearly everyone I met in Russia was introduced as a "specialist". This word eventually became rather exhausting. The qualification for the status was that one had undergone a short course in something or other—poultry keeping or plumbing or what not—at the local State technical institution. But what a refreshing change that was from England, where in my experience people could with difficulty be persuaded to take any courses at all, and even when they did, nobody thought much the more about them.

I returned to England convinced of the strength and genuineness of the Russian experiment. But though this visit had been an illumination in itself, it sharpened, if anything, my sense of isolation from my English surroundings. Ordinary responsible people in England, the people with whom one worked day by day, could not be expected to take an interest in lines of thought which cut across or carried one beyond, the rather limited boundaries of the usual religion or politics. Out of kindness they would listen for a short while, but they thought it necessary to make it clear quite soon, that this type of thing was unorthodox, and, indeed dangerous; and must not be entertained for any length of time, or at all seriously. I knew quite well from experience in the selection of children for higher education that only 10 per cent. of the population were fit to occupy controlling positions (that, by the way, is about the proportion that officers bear to other ranks in the armed forces, and they are forced to take realities into consideration) and I knew also that the stability of English society, ever since the days of the Tudors, had been due to the Radical policy of taking that 10 per cent. into the upper classes. But it was nevertheless necessary to see that the conditions of the ninety were reasonable, and this had been terribly neglected. How amazing it was in 1941, to find suddenly that to mention Russia had actually become respectable. In 1935 it was interesting, though sad, to trace the limits within which one could bring up social questions. The public social services did in fact employ a considerable number of officials; these officials reported to monthly meetings of committees and sub-committees of the large Local Authorities—the County and County Borough Councils—and these committees sanctioned such expenditure as they thought necessary to meet the conditions the officials reported to them. There were certain central financial and other controls in the responsible Ministries in London, but at that time these committees of Local Authorities had a very important voice in deciding the scale of many of the main social services—Poor

Relief, Housing, Public Health and Education among them. Very few Authorities indeed had a Socialist majority, so few that their names were well known; and the ordinary Authority normally fought a steady battle to keep down expenditure within the limits that were politically possible. Generally, indeed, it was the London Ministries that pressed for greater activity, and the officials used the London circulars to induce the Authorities to move forward; they were, however, employed and paid by the Authorities and not by London, and the scope for manoeuvre was somewhat limited. In my experience, Authorities were always willing to listen to factual statements. The best official was really one who kept his Authority fully informed, but did not propose expenditure which the Authority would consider extravagant. This was reasonable on two accounts: in the first place it was obvious to all concerned that municipal finance was already strained to near breaking point, and in the second it was obvious, at least to officials, that the situation could not really be met by a policy of redistributing through taxation the profits made by those who were able to extract them from the social system as it then existed. If the position were to be put right at all, it could only be done by some radical measures, involving the nationalization of the land and of certain sectors of finance and industry, and by the introduction of "production for use", at any rate within certain limits. The ordinary responsible official, therefore, kept his eyes open but his mouth largely shut. He would usually be able to come to some real understanding with his Chairman, and, with many of the more influential members of his committee, but it could only be on the basis that the work of the Authority must be largely palliative, and even that on little more than a minor scale. In fact, in the circumstances of the day, it was clear that national economic diseases could not be tackled without national action.

This framework was not really as unsatisfactory as it sounds. Short of armed revolution it was clear that progress could only be made by a process of "educating" the public, helping them to see for themselves what was wrong, and to recognize the principles on which an advance could take place. The official had unrivalled opportunities to observe the facts, and in his committee he had the advantage of meeting men and women most of whom were at least disposed to become acquainted with realities and who, in their turn, were willing to accept his help in the difficult task of presenting these conceptions to the public and in the meantime, there was clearly some value in a certain number of small-scale experiments in what might be called social engineering. The raw material, in the shape of the bulk of the dispossessed classes, was clearly exceedingly intractable, and there was much to be learnt about its reactions to anything but the standard treatment. This was the period, it will be recalled, of the experimental housing estates in Holland. Similar experiments, in education as in other branches of the social services, were going on in England;

one might quote the "Village Colleges" of Cambridge-shire and the housing trusts of Kensington. Nevertheless, as the decade progressed, I found myself driven increasingly near despair. The fundamental difficulty was the inertia of the dispossessed themselves. In Southampton in 1935, as I have already said, we had ten thousand unemployed upon the registers of the Ministry of Labour. The Town Council had made a substantial area of allotment land available for the men, but few would take up a plot. They seemed to prefer to spend their days in the Club smoking (subsidized) cigarettes and drinking cups of (subsidized) tea. The land was necessarily at some distance from the docks and it was thought that perhaps more use would be made of it if a building could be provided on the allotment which would give shelter in rain and a place to wash, and eat, and to keep tools and seeds. A Labour Councillor who was a building contractor and a very kindly person, offered to provide the whole of the materials needed, including all the fittings, and drive them there in his own lorries—on the one condition that some of the unemployed carpenters, bricklayers and plumbers in the club would volunteer to erect the building in their all too ample "leisure" time. It seems difficult to believe after all these years, but the men refused to do the work. They said they ought to be paid trade union rates of wages for the job. The materials lay rotting in the rain until the Councillor, in disgust, sent his lorries to pick them up again.

It seemed to me, whenever we touched the really poor

(and they were so many) that they were already too far gone to renew the struggle. I could not detect any power to take even political action, let alone revolutionary action. The electorate returned Conservative governments with remorseless fidelity. I wrote to the headquarters of the Communist Party of Great Britain and asked them what was their policy in the circumstances. I have their reply still, typed in brown ink on a yellow sheet of paper. It was to the effect that they did not propose to put any constructive policy before the people; there was nothing at this stage which could be done except only to agitate, and ceaselessly to harp upon the miseries of the present situation. It seemed that Hitler was not far wrong, and that our society must inevitably shortly, collapse. I thankfully acknowledge now that in making that estimate I was astray. The real truth was proved, first by the war, and secondly by the General Election of 1945.

CHAPTER SEVENTEEN

BATTERSEA BRIDGE

"Habemus autem thesaurum istum in vasis fictilbus"
2 COR. 4

With the declaration of war in 1939, the balance of affairs was radically altered. My own work had clearly to remain in abeyance at least "for the duration". These tales, it will be understood, are not intended to be an account of my own life, but merely of certain events or movements with which I was lucky enough to be connected in those strange years between the end of the first war and the end of the second; and if, therefore, anything which I have said has raised any slight feeling of curiosity as to what happened next to any of the characters, including myself, I beg to be excused if I have not said enough to satisfy it. Perhaps whatever I I had written on certain subjects might have been read with some interest; but it is not easy to write about some things and others are not adventures at all in the usual sense, though they certainly from time to time "come upon" one, if I may so translate from the derivation of the word.

May I then say no more, by way of introduction to this last story, than what follows. My war service fell into three parts. My time with the mines, 1940-41, led

L*   163

up to three years over which I was chosen to act as Secretary to a new Admiralty inter-departmental committee on anti-submarine weapons. During that time, this Committee, which consisted of naval officers, scientists and manufacturers, was called upon first to design and then bring into manufacture on a large scale, an entirely new range of anti-submarine weapons, under the tremendous weight of a very serious attack upon our shipping. It is obviously impracticable for me to describe in any detail the problems which we had to face or our reasons for the action we took, though it will be realized that the subject was, and still is, of the profoundest importance to the history of England. It would be impossible even to attempt to name those who played the most constructive parts in that extraordinary mental adventure, the end of which even from the newspapers, it is clear is not yet. But I must name one character well known to the public before the war as an occupant of the extreme right wing in politics, a man of very great distinction, who deserves the deepest gratitude and admiration on account of his connection with these matters, for the perhaps somewhat unexpected reason that, in a most influential position, he agreed to do nothing. At one crucial point in the discussions Lord Cherwell said he would be present. He was then acting as special scientific adviser to the Premier, who was naturally very closely concerned. I and a few others, who considered ourselves on the side of the angels, had been informed that Lord Cherwell had come to the meeting determined to secure a certain course of action. From his face as he entered the Committee I feared that that was indeed so.

In actual fact, like his great opponent, Mr. Bevin, on an earlier occasion in the Macmillan Committee on Finance and Industry, he composed himself to listen with absolute impartiality to what the witnesses had to say. At the close of the statements, he got up with the briefest of comments, "Gentlemen," he said, "I think there is no need for me to intervene," and in another second he was gone. He must have intervened in a different sense afterwards, for from that moment onwards our way was made as easy as those in the highest quarters could make it.

Anti-submarine weapons cannot be considered in the void apart from the question of the ships which have to carry them and in particular to carry their ammunition. It was on this Committee that I made the acquaintance of Mr. Cole, Assistant Director of Naval Construction, to whom I owe many kindnesses and, in the end, my third and in some ways my most interesting war-time assignment, an appointment to the Control Commission for Germany. This appointment, which carried the rank of Brigadier, involved being in charge of the control and liquidation of all German stocks of underwater weapons, torpedoes, mines, depth charges and the like and gear associated with them. In the first weeks I was frequently called upon to represent the Trade and Economics Division of the Commission in the discussions on the demolition of shipyards and armaments factories in Germany and it was interesting, though aggravating, to observe how difficult it seemed to be for some people to understand that it was only in the exceptional case that a line could be drawn between what was and what was not, at least potentially, an armaments factory. From what has been said earlier in these stories, it will be clear, for example, that a clock-making factory is also potentially a bomb fuse factory and what we had to explain was that the question at issue was not how many "armaments factories" should be pulled down but how many *factories*, whatever their nature, must necessarily be left standing if German civilian life was to be allowed to go on at all. Fortunately for me in this case, I was instructed to put a foot down.

However, six months had scarcely passed when I was invited on behalf of the Ethiopian Government to go out to Addis Ababa to act as the Emperor's Adviser on Education. During the years in which I had been initiated into large-scale manufacture I had come to understand better and at first-hand the nature of industry as opposed to commerce, the place of manufacture in the economic machine, its relations with scientists and research workers and the function of the various levels in its hierarchy. What I had not grasped so well was the dependence of industry upon roots in earlier stages of the development of a country. I had formed the view that within limits a measure of industrialization was necessary in our Colonial territories if their standards of living were to be raised or indeed if we were to retain the Empire, for which we had just been fighting, at all; and when I was asked to go out to Ethiopia and advise on educational development, I made up my mind that here was my chance to experiment with the introduction of manufacture in a backward country. The available commercial information showed that Ethiopia had an adverse trade balance which was largely caused by the import of textiles, though the country possessed areas suited to the growing of cotton, and, indeed, the Italians, during their brief occupation, had actually set up ginneries in one area and had made a start with the spinning and weaving of cotton in Dire Dawa on the railway line for Djibouti to Addis Ababa.

But the adventures in Ethiopia are really "another story". Suffice it to say that when I reached Addis Ababa as early as the end of 1945, I found that people were inclined to consider that England, as a Great Power, was finished. This was a difficult conception for one who had served through an apparently victorious war to appreciate. However, their information was good. England is not rotten, but it is in a difficult patch and Englishmen in general do not seem to be very good at reading writing on walls. Some of the institutions in which my generation was brought up are failing. Cruttwell, Principal of my college at Oxford, was always particularly incensed in a book by any passage which began "I believe . . ." "Huh!" he would snort, "I see we have reached the Credo." The suggestion was that the unfortunate author had now passed the stage at which his assertions could be proved by evidence; and they must accordingly be worthless. I must say I have since found in life that this is usually the case. The other rule he gave the would-be writer was "Never Narrate". I have so sadly broken the second rule in this book that at all costs I must now avoid breaking the first one. I will, instead, ask my readers whether they do not themselves consider that four in particular of our first-class institutions are visibly in various stages of fundamental transformation—the Church, the Empire, the Balance of Trade and the Armed Services; and that to use the mildest language it seems to be of vital importance to England that as many people as possible should apply themselves now to examining the state of these institutions, if only in order to preserve as many of our number as possible from starvation?

"We have this treasure in earthen vessels."

Like Dives in the Parable, I think I should abandon the attempt to send messages to my brethren; yet I would like to tell one last tale, if only because it might help to illustrate for the children that thoughtful nursery line,

"Things aren't always what they seem."

Before dawn one day in the winter of 1940, the telephone by my bedside rang: I was requested to go and see what could be done with a mine at Battersea Bridge. The mine was reported to have fallen on the Southern electric railway, and all trains in and out of London were being held up until the obstruction could be cleared.

Always a little uncertain of the geography of London south of the river, I left my driver to take the shortest route. A thin rain was falling, it was dark, cold and rather foggy, the tramlines were greasy and the whole situation was as unpleasant as it could well be. In such light as the headlamps threw, the usual shattered buildings bore witness to the force of the raid of the last few hours. I ran up the stairs of the deserted station, made for the ticket office, found the station master and asked him to show me the mine.

We set off up the railway in a northerly direction towards Westminster. I was surprised at the width of the track. As we stumbled along the ballast by the side of the line the first miserable grey light began to break; shrouded in a wet mackintosh I felt hot and cold in turns. The water from my sleeves was wetting my wrists. There was a siding on the left and, as we approached the point where the lines diverged and it was necessary to start stepping over the rails, the station master came to a halt. "We're nearly there, sir," he said. "I think I shall leave you now".

I could see absolutely nothing to indicate the presence of a mine. I caught his arm and pressed for further directions. Pointing up the track he indicated a covered waggon some way along the siding. "It's under there, sir," he said, in a voice which had sunk to a whisper and, turning on his heel, he departed in the direction of the station.

Tuckwell and I looked at each other a little glumly. It was obviously impossible that a mine ten feet long and weighing a ton, could come down, either with or without a parachute, roll under a truck and not even tear up the railway. The only possible explanation was that the mine had come down with a crash, its parachute shot off by anti-aircraft fire; it must have buried itself in the track and the waggon must then have been shunted over it before its presence was discovered. This was in itself an exceedingly nasty state of affairs. It would probably be necessary to move the truck to get at the mine at all, and the act of moving the truck at this stage might very well activate a fuse. There should be no difficulty in towing the truck off at the end of a long cable, once the cable had been fixed; and if "damage could have been accepted", that would have been the sensible way to set about the matter, but it was clearly up to us, if possible, to prevent the mine from detonating at all.

We walked on carefully trying, as we got near the truck, to avoid stumbling on the loose ballast. As my head went slowly forward, my eyes glued to the dark area under the truck, the rain suddenly shot down my neck. Absolutely no indication of the presence of a mine was to be seen. We drew level with the truck; I went down on hands and knees on some dirty black cinders, and peered gingerly in between the wheels. I noticed that as my elbows took my weight they were trembling.

There in the centre of the track, right under the truck, was a little grey aluminium parachute flare, about eighteen inches long, with a delicate white silk parachute attached. I had made it a rule to take no unnecessary risks; I didn't know exactly how these flares worked so

I unhitched the parachute as a memento and returned gravely to the station. "The trains can run now, station master," I said; "It is only a parachute flare. You might get the A.R.P. to come and take that away sometime."

Date Due

NOV 1 8 '59			
DEC 2 '59			
MR 6 '61			
JE 26'61			
AG 14 '6			
OC 5 '70			

ⒼⒷ   PRINTED   IN U. S. A.